STANDING TALL

Acquiring The 13 Riches
of Life Effortlessly

"If you're lucky to be one of the few to find someone who will tolerate you…"

Barenaked Ladies

I'm one of the lucky few. The Fabulous Davene, my bride, makes Job, the guy in the Bible, look impatient. Without you, this book would never have been written.
While the list of things you bring us daily is virtually endless, the priceless gift that overwhelms me was your belief in me and circling the wagons when we lost it all and were flat broke. And I wish all of you, kind enough to read this tale, the same kind of unshakeable belief and support I came to know.

Chapter One

A Fable?

There's an old saying, "facts should never get in the way of a good yarn."

Did the Red Sea really part? Did Buddha really find enlightenment under the Bodhi tree? Did the great fish really swallow Jonah?

Have these stories survived because they are priceless metaphorical fables to those with insight, or did they really happen? Most people are skeptical cynics. Any hint of suspicion makes them dubious, and, so, they reject the entire message.

I mention this, because, as this tale of Seven Ancient Verities and a Map was being told to me by Doc—likeable as he was—my skepticism quickly bordered on disbelief. Have you ever wanted something to be true, but, try as you may, you have a really hard time believing it? I was told that the Seven Ancient Verities and a Map to the 13 Riches of Life that I am about to share with you had been passed from person to person, handwritten by the passer of them, for over 4,000 years.

To me, the passing of these Verities from one person to another for centuries, well, that was unimaginable. Just wait… it gets even more taxing on the old belief meter. Allegedly, those who embrace the Verities and work through them as instructed can then understand the attached Map to the 13 Riches of Life… each then acquires great wealth in all areas of their life. My blogging peers knew nothing about it—there were no written records of the Map to the 13 Riches of Life anywhere. My research turned up virtually nothing… just a few obscure hints that seemed to suggest that the Verities existed and that "the wealth thing"—whatever that meant— was true. I noticed, oddly, that I was conflicted. Hope versus cynicism.

In today's world of quick fixes, instant gratification, and promises of pixie-dust self-help solutions for all that ails us for attending a weekend seminar and the unmet promises that invariably follow, skepticism is at an all-time high. I can't blame you if you're skeptical. I was, even when Verities were passed to me.

Mired in debt and desperation, I hawked what I could to get a plane ticket and I headed to Kauai, Hawaii. I wanted to meet with a guy who left a comment on a blog I had written. I will go into in more detail later. I did not know about the Ancient Verities until we met at his home. Within a year, my debt and desperation was replaced with peace and prosperity. Today, I live on Kauai, a far cry from a one-bedroom apartment in Seabrook, New Hampshire. Occasionally, I have a hard time believing that I get paid for what I love to do… but it is true. And the 13 Riches? Yes, they keep pouring in. Those are the facts.

I'm a little ahead of myself, so let me go back to the very beginning. Here's how it happened…

Chapter Two

The Lanai

Why won't you tell me?" Doc asked. Toni was silent.

"Why?" Doc asked again, controlling his voice, so as not to shout. "Why? Why won't you tell me how you became so wealthy?" This time, hewas unsuccessful. Doc was shouting into the phone.

Toni remained calm and explained, for the second time, why she was not yet willing to share what she had done to become so successful financially.

"Look, I'm not saying 'no'. Just not yet. The value of this relationship, this friendship is something I'm not willing to risk, and, right now, that's exactly what it feels like."

"Why does it feel like a risk to you? I'm the one at risk, Toni. My pay has been cut by 25 percent, and another 25 percent is going to vanish ninety days from now. I'm suddenly raising both kids on my own, and…"

"Doc. Stop!" she raised her voice a tad, to interrupt Doc's rant.

He kept rambling about his troubles, but he had heard her order to stop, and his voice trailed off about two-thirds of the way through the list of negative circumstances.

"Keep asking and keep working your business," Toni said in a soft and encouraging way. "Just know that, one day, you will be able to stand tall and wealthy in all areas of life, a fearless victor, no longer a fearful victim."

I asked Doc if that was how he remembered the conversation, or if he had just generalized the conversation. He sat silently for a while. A long while. I began to feel anxious and was unsure if I should speak. It's hard to say, that first time, how long the silence was, but I came to understand that Doc was someone who thought before he spoke.

The anxiousness passed. Became uncomfortable. Have you ever been in a situation in which you don't know if you should speak, change the subject, or ask the same question again? I caved and repeated the question. Almost.

He raised his hand slightly as I began to speak and looked out from the lanai. He pointed and asked, "Does the ocean look bigger to you… bigger than other times you've look at it?"

I nodded. He smiled and kept looking out at the sea. I was somewhat relieved to have a break from the piercing eye contact that he made with me from the moment I had arrived. It was not so much piercing as deep. When he looked at me, he was looking into my eyes, never shifting his.

"Did you know that is the largest coffee plantation in the United States? Right here on Kauai, right there," his voice rose with childlike enthusiasm. "I guess all colors are wonderful, but there is something about that green of those coffee fields running into that massive blue ocean that just does something inside of me…"

"I'm not sure I am getting what you are really saying, but it feels like you are telling me something, Doc. Are you?" I asked.

"Did you know coffee is actually in the Gardenia family?" Doc said. I opened my mouth to speak, but he wasn't done.

"It's intoxicating to drive through those coffee fields when they are flowering. It's a theory I have about why people get tired here around 8:00 at night. And, yes, I'm sharing something with you, Mark."

"And that is?"

"Most people, when you ask them about the great moments in their lives, share them well enough, but, if you listen closely, you can tell they were not fully present while that great moment was happening," Doc said. "Just be here with this moment, in the moment. And, yes, that is word-for-word between me and Toni."

Chapter Three

20 Hours Earlier

The pilot announced that we were coming into Kauai from the south side, and, if we looked out the windows on the left side of the plane, we would see the "Garden Isle".

I noticed the excitement within me was building, and I found myself standing up in the aisle and looking out the windows. I had done a reasonable amount of flying over the past three years, and I must admit that the attitudes of the passengers on this flight were far different than those I had been witness to on past flights. The cheerfulness and chatter on the flight from Seattle had annoyed me. Hey, I was preoccupied: I wanted to be ready for my big interview with a subject who had traditionally avoided the media.

My best guess, now, is that I just could not figure out why he said "yes" to me. Rumor had it he was "out there" and basically reclusive. I guess the happiness, anticipation, and excitement the passengers were experiencing felt like interruptions, messing with my concentration. Now, I know better. I know it was self-centered fear. I missed a lot of wonderful energy because I simply was thinking about the future—the interview—and not being in the moment.

It was my first trip to Hawaii, and, while I'd done some research online, nothing could prepare me for the view out the window. Ocean, mountains, and the jungle… I got a short break from myself and my fears, and I allowed myself to enjoy my mounting excitement.

It didn't last long. We touched down, and I got my rental car and headed to the Sheraton on the south side of the island. I checked in and was pleasantly surprised to have been upgraded to an oceanfront room. There was a fruit basket in the room from Doc and his wife with a note that made me smile:

> *"Enjoy the view and fruit. Relax, it's all good.*
> *Our home is only about 20 minutes away.*
> *There's a map in the envelope.*

Chapter Four

One Week Earlier

"Did this recluse tell you why he invited you to Kauai?" my close friend, Joanne, asked with a dismissive look, as she knocked back a little more wine. Ouch.

"Sort of," I mumbled. I had a pretty good idea of what was coming next. It did.

"What the hell does that friggin' mean?" Joanne was earthy. She was cynical. She was judgmental and harsh. "Is he paying your way there?"

"No," I said, breaking eye contact. She wasn't off-target in her concern. My bank account status? Miserable.

Joanne was a close friend. When I shared with her that I had been invited to Kauai, I asked her to dig deep on this guy Doc, to get past the normal stuff found on page one of Google. She was good at that and I wanted her to dig deeper so I'd be prepared. When I first put it out there, she yawned. Intentionally. Loudly. She used a lot of exaggerated body language to express herself. Above all, for some reason, I've never understood, Joanne was protective of me.

"What do you mean, 'sort of'? I mean, you're a freelance writer, and your articles sell for how much? On average, what the frig do you get for an article?"

She knew it was $300 to $800. I said nothing, just looked down at my shoe tops.

"So, this clown, who you say never gives interviews about succeeding, asked you to come over at your own expense? I'm not getting it. If it's a great article, if there is something so special in the article, and someone buys it, you still lose money? You're broke, idiot."

My mind began racing, debating. I thought, *She'll rip me up one side and down the other if I share what Doc said may happen.* Sharing hopes or dreams with Joanne, I had learned, was not a good idea when she was in her protective mode.

Chapter Five

Several Months Earlier

Six months earlier.

At the time preceding my visit to Doc, my blog about working from home with sales companies and online businesses averaged 15 to 30 comments each week. The overall theme of my blog is that, while some people do well with network marketing companies, direct sales companies, and online businesses, the overall track record of successes vs. failures is a poor one.

In one blog post, I shared some figures from the DSA (Direct Selling Association), and some additional statistics that I had compiled. In the post, I used the statistics to illustrate that while people *can* succeed, very few people actually *do* succeed. Most people who blog for a living or try to build a following to make their freelance articles become more marketable know that writing in such a way that encourages and invites comments about things people are passionate about is the smart play.

This particular blog post had considerably more comments than the rest of my posts. Most of the comments were from people who were in some kind of home-based business, and each of them explained why their deal was different, better, or the one that works. A good chunk of the other comments gave me a ringing endorsement for exposing the odds and how dismal the chances of success are. Others were angry skeptics and believers in the American Dream, slugging it out.

As I was reading through the comments that day, I came across one that really intrigued me. It read:

....

I appreciate the post. Your information about the success rate is accurate, but not true. While there will always be good, bad, and indifferent companies people can partner with, along with the normal cast of hustlers and con artists out there, the truth is that people have decided, unconsciously, to fail or succeed, before they even pull out their credit card to join. Their internal blueprint has predetermined the outcome.

This includes, of course, the original choice of

what to join. Keep up the good work, and dig a little
deeper if you want to be great. Information and truth
are not the same thing.

....

My attention was piqued. I wanted to know who the commenter was. The commenter turned out to be a guy named Doc, who allegedly made some noise and big bucks working for himself in home-based businesses. I started snooping around and found countless videos on YouTube, two blogs, and two decent websites. He was very active online. His YouTube channel, which features tips about working from home, had over 500,000 views. I figured he was just another slick peddler, making comments like that on lots of blogs to get people curious and draw them to his site, so he would be able to sell them his "secrets". Pretty common practice.

I was just about to bounce off his website, when I noticed something odd. I didn't see a "product" page promoting anything for sale which is damn unusual for a blog of any kind. I became curious, figuring that I had missed some kind of links to buy books, or CDs, or some other product. I jumped from page to page, but I found nothing of the kind. I looked further, pouring over several months worth of Doc's posts to find a sales pitch somewhere within his blog. Still, I found nothing.

Instead what I found in going back through his posts was a wealth of videos, in which Doc was teaching something very specific. It wasn't general stuff, rehashing simple ideas, nor did it have your typical motivational fare, just plain language content. It was confrontational and in-your-face. It really challenged what was normally taught about earning income. The two hallmarks of his videos were common sense and personal responsibility.

Then, I noticed something else even more interesting. There had not been anything new for a couple of years. I hopped over to a site that rated and ranked network marketing home-based business blogs. I saw the usual list of characters at the top, and knowing who most of them were, I knew that they all spent money advertising their blogs. Scrolling down, I saw that Doc's blog ranked 18th worldwide, and was accompanied by this blurb:

....

This blog contains more VALUABLE content than any
other Network Marketing blog on the Internet. More free
skills than anyone will ever need and they run free courses.
Life-changing courses...

Now, I was getting curious. Free? Everything?

I headed over to http://masterkeyexperience.com, another site of Doc's that was linked to the lazy networker site. As I made my way to his other site, I was certain that that would be where I found products and courses for sale. I thought, *AHA! There is a course offered there! I get it: he gives them some stuff, lets them try it out and get a taste of what he is offering, and, then, he leads them to this site, where he sells to them.*

Feeling hot on the trail, I clicked on the page about the course and found out it's only offered once a year. The description of the course says that it is six months of daily work that helps people learn to help themselves. The text below the videos asserts that virtually all self-help books and seminars with big promises are a waste of time, that slogans won't make you successful, and that only hard mental labor can bring success and abundance. It was refreshingly blunt in pointing out that change is a challenge, and most people won't do the work.

Next, I read something that still blows me away. The site said that all of the people accepted for MasterKeyExperience program come into it on a scholarship. The scholarship is pre-paid for them by the previous members. It costs the people scholarshipped just one dollar. During the course the new members decide what it is worth to them, if anything and can "pay-it-forward" for the following year… or not. Huh?!

I thought, *Who **is** this guy?*

As I look deeper into both sites, I see videos of Doc and his wife living in Kauai, living his dream, and, they are apparently doing so, despite having websites with nothing for sale. I wondered, *How is this guy earning a living?*

We've all seen thousands of sites claiming to have "life-changing" information (for sale, of course), with testimonials attesting to the magic of the program. Instead, what I found on Doc's site said just the opposite. It said, that "no one can change anyone's life" and that "The wisdom and knowledge needed to change and be successful unilaterally is already within each of us." The site described how people make changes within and create different outcomes, creating new realities for themselves. And—get this—it said that the new reality did not come about through massive action and that massive action is, in fact, a total waste of time.

What happened next stunned me. The site said, "Don't take my word for it; read some of the stories for yourself." I clicked a link, expecting to see the normal five to ten testimonials of raving fans. What I found, instead, was links to hundreds and hundreds and hundreds of blogs. Doc suggested, in a short video, to pick a few of these blogs, go back to "Week One" on any of the blogs, and follow the journey of some of the bloggers over the course of 26 weeks.

I read about challenges, struggles, victories, and defeats that each of them faced. I read about how overwhelmed Doc's students became with all the work they had to do to maintain their scholarship, and, as the blog entries progressed through their journeys, I read how they began to adapt and feel confident. I read about change, pride, effort, and the ups and downs they experienced. I was hit with the realization that what I was actually reading were accounts of the human spirit being challenged and, then, meeting the challenge.

Around 700 people who had gone through the Master Key Experience had made an entry once a week for 26 weeks or more. There were over 20,000 posts raving about this course. People from all over the world, posting weekly from dozens of countries on five different continents, were working hard and affecting change in their lives. For not the first time that day, I thought, *Who the hell is this guy?*

What would get that many people to write weekly, sharing intimate details of their struggles? The taglines on the site were #MasterKey Experience and #NothingLikeIt.

What would get so many people to write weekly? What could this "experience" be triggering to cause all of those people to open their hearts and souls and vulnerabilities to the world? A thorough check of all the big self-helpers and motivational speakers online showed that there is nothing on the planet that had this type of universal endorsement in such copious numbers. Clearly, as the tagline said, there was "nothing like it" that I'd ever seen online. Again, I returned to my mind's common refrain for the day, *And it's a buck? Who the hell is this guy?*

I got to thinking...*over 20,000 endorsements? Can this be right? I'm reading 26-week story after 26-week story of how people are making changes in their lives, their relationships, and doing better in business.* Equally fascinating was that blogs weren't hailing Doc as a guru or that there is some "secret" or "magic"... they all seemed to be getting improvement through their own efforts and feeling great about it. At this point, my curiosity was overwhelming.

As I read the journeys of the many bloggers and read about the changes they were implementing in their lives, my own financial struggles and failures in relationships caused my curiosity to burn still stronger. My mind racing at warp-speed, I knew I had to find a way to get an interview. I knew it would be a great interview, but I must confess, I also wanted to know how it was that people were making changes. I needed to make some myself.

My research only turned up a single interview with the inimitable Doc. One! Not encouraging. I found videos of him interviewing lots people from the lanai at his home, but only one interview with the man, himself. Undeterred, I reached out and asked him for a live, face-to-face interview.

My email requesting an interview led to a series of email exchanges over the next six months.

Dear Doc,

Thank you for your recent comment on my blog post about the potential success and failure rate for people working home-based businesses. I was particularly intrigued by your statement that a person's success or failure is determined before they even pull out their credit card to join.

I'd love to learn more about how and why you feel that way. Of even greater interest to my 10,000 readers would be how you went from bankrupt to beachfront, as you claim on the videos. People want to know what you did to get what you got. Of this, I am most certain. That would be one question for sure, "What did you do to get what you got?"

I also believe the exposure will help more people learn about your Master Key Experience course. Saying 'yes' to an interview will inform and help our thousands of readers; of this, I am also certain.

Sincerely, Mark

I received the following response fairly quickly, about 2 days: Aloha Mark, Appreciate you reaching out. I don't leave Kauai, so an interview would have to be here. While I like your writing style and have followed your blog for a while and commend you on choosing professionalism over sensationalism, there are two things standing in our way of getting together.

One: Asking what we did to get what we got is the wrong question. It's a question people who've decided to fail tend to ask. It won't help your readers.

Two: I don't do interviews. If you can't figure out the right question, that would make you the wrong person to get together with for what I have in mind.

Fix point one first.

Keep giving to keep growing, Believe,

Doc

Five Months Earlier

Dear Doc,

It feels like you want me to figure something out and, yet, on your sites, I get the clear impression you think games about serious things are bullshit.

Are you saying that if we can work things out that we'll get together and it will be more than an interview?

Sincerely,
Mark

He replied:

Aloha Mark,

Yes.

Keep giving to keep growing,
Believe, Doc

Four Months Earlier

Dear Doc,

In your first email, you said you liked my style. Are we talking

about a book or something like that?

Sincerely,
Mark

He replied: Aloha Mark,

LMAO. What would "something like that" in describing a book be? Keep giving to keep growing,

Believe,

Doc

Three months earlier

Dear Doc,

I guess "sort of a book thing" is dumb. Have I lost points for style?

Sincerely,
Mark

He replied: Aloha Mark,

Yes, you've lost points for style, but gained points for humor and humility.

Keep giving to keep growing, Believe,
Doc

Two Months Earlier

Dear Doc,

I guess the only thing standing in the way of getting together for an interview that isn't an interview and to do something, "sort of a book thing" is all on me. I'm avoiding what question to ask, instead of "What did you do to get what you got?"

Would you be willing to help me figure that out?

Sincerely,
Mark

His return

Aloha Mark,

Yes.

Keep giving to keep growing,

Believe,
Doc

One Month Earlier

Dear Doc,

Your last email was difficult to understand, very wordy. ☺

I'm not sure what the next step is, but, after spending some time on your site, I believe I know what my readers need to know to be more successful.

It's the be-do-have part, right?

It's not "What did you do to get what you got?" That's the wrong question.

One has to 'be' a different person, so they can do different things which will let them have different things, seems to be the essence of what you are sharing.

So, I'm going to ask you, "How do we 'be' a different person, yet retain who we really are?"

Sincerely,

Mark

He replied:

Aloha Mark,

Impressed.

So I've got this message, and I need someone of your writing style to frame this message in a story. See, if you want to become famous, this isn't going to work. The message needs to be the star, not the writer, nor me. We're after a galaxy of people who become heroes in their own lives, not a star.

If you understand the message, it will make you wealthy in all areas of your life, not just financially. For many reasons, you need to write it with a pen-name. More on this when we chat on my lanai. I'm not leaving the island, as you know.

In or out?

Keep giving to keep growing,

Believe,
Doc

Twenty-Nine Days Earlier

Dear Doc,

In.

Sincerely,
Mark

He replied:

Aloha Mark,

See you in a month.

Keep giving to keep growing,

Believe,
Doc

And so began my own journey, as well as this book that you are currently reading.

Chapter Six

One Week Earlier

That day when my cynical, harsh, self-appointed protector Joanne stopped by my tiny apartment with her research, I could feel her glaring at me. Uncomfortably, I diverted my gaze to my shoe tops. She had repeated, mega-loudly, "So this clown, who you say never gives interviews about succeeding, asks you to come over at your own expense? I'm not getting it. If it's a great article, if there is something so special in it, and someone buys it, you still lose money?"

"It may be something like, ah, sort of a book," I said, surprising Joanne — and even myself—with the firmness in my voice.

"Really?" She leaned forward, eyes soft.

I was shocked. Joanne mistrusted just about everybody, and she didn't like most people. I had expected her to yell at me for being a cock-eyed optimist, as she had done so many times before.

"What did you find out about this guy?" I asked.

"I'll tell you this first; he is not a popular guy with a lot of the people selling tools, leads, live events, and so forth in the home-based business market. The more I dug around about this guy, the more unpopular your guy, Doc, seems to be with that crowd. And, apparently, the self-helpers who know about him really don't like him, either." Joanne paused. Then she smiled and said, "I like him."

"Why?" I allowed myself to feel the sparkle of optimistic excitement. Like I said, Joanne didn't like anyone.

"I researched the guys and gals and companies he isn't popular with. Not being liked by them is a compliment for people who have authentic ethics," Joanne said. "You know, that crowd of pied-pipers who sell secrets and motivational drivel... from my perspective, not being liked by them says something good."

She had about five or six groups of papers stapled together inside a folder. Going to Kauai became a no-brainer for me. The self-doubt and second-guessing the financial outlay vanished. She opened the folder and gave me a quick breakdown of what each set covered about Doc, and, then, she zipped them into my computer travel case. I grinned, relief and excitement rushing through me. To top it off, she gave me one of her rare, reassuring smiles. It wasn't until I started looking at them on the plane that I found the $500 she had stapled to the back of one of her reports.

Chapter Seven

Back to the Lanai

ʃor reasons you'll understand shortly, the names of the characters and some of the circumstances have been changed. Some have been changed to meet the objective of sharing this with you in print, to develop a galaxy of wealthy stars and avoid making Doc a be-all-end-all super star guru. Why am I telling you this now, rather than at the beginning? To help push readers, like you, into a deeper understanding of where riches really are born; within. You'll find that by placing principles over personalities in your own life, you become the star, the hero of your own life.

One thing Doc had emailed wasn't completely clear to me, and I want to clear that up first. One of the emails stated I'd get wealthy in all areas of life, if I understood and applied the message. I *did* become wealthy in all areas of my life. When I first read that email, I assumed that such a feat would be complex. It was not. I thought it would take a long time. It did not. What Doc did not mention was that the challenge was not about just being able to understand the message. It was to understand completely enough to act on it instantly.

Doc and I sat on his lanai, looking out over the coffee fields at the magnificent, vast ocean. The person who had taught Doc the information that he was about to introduce to me had declined sharing with Doc what he had asked her for: her fast-track to big income.

"So… Toni denied sharing this message with you, because she felt it would threaten the relationship?" I asked.

"Risk. She felt it would put the relationship at risk," he clarified in an authoritative manner. It seemed like the distinction was important to Doc, but, at the time, I must admit that I did not understand the difference.

"Right, risk. And this wasn't the first time you had asked her to share this secret about success with you and not the first time she declined, right?"

He looked me dead in the eye, and I felt something I'd never felt. There was this feeling of compassion oozing around me. Doc offered a slight smile, one that was knowing, yet sad. It lasted only a few seconds, but it was one of those times in life when a few moments in time can feel interminable. His head turned back towards the ocean, and I knew we'd be entering into another period of very long silence...and very loud silence for me.

After what seemed like ten minutes, Doc finally broke the silence, "What are you feeling?" His voice was soft, but, somehow, it rang loudly in my ears. Maybe it just startled me after so much silence.

"I'm feeling curious about the sadness I saw in that smile—in your eyes, I guess—just before you turned towards the ocean," I said.

He pointed out that curious isn't a *feeling*. "What are you feeling? Can you describe it?"

I didn't know if Doc's wanting to know how I felt was manipulative, insightful, or what... but I broke eye contact and silently looked out over the lush scenery.

"I'm not sure what I am feeling, Doc," I finally responded, "but I know I am curious about why you looked sort of sad when you smiled after I asked you about Toni declining to share her secrets of success with you."

"There are no secrets to success," Doc said. "It makes me a little sad to know so many people believe that there are secrets or some mystery to all the riches in life." I was beginning to notice a pattern. If his hand touched the side of his face, there was more coming. In this case, the floodgates were about to open... "That's why you're here though, right? We're going to fix all that and create amazing wealth with your 'sort of like a book' thing, yes?"

Shocked. Stunned. Was Doc saying I was going to write a book? Was something I had been hoping for suddenly dropping into my lap? Is this what it feels like when hope begins to move towards reality? Saying that my mind started racing would be an understatement.

I didn't know how to describe the matrix of thoughts and emotions swirling within me, so I retreated to the topic of the secrets of success. "Before we change the world, can you tell me why you believe there are no secrets to success? Isn't that what you were asking Toni about Doc?"

"I guess it would be fair to say that who I was then would be grouped in with millions of people who believed there were secrets to success, that wealth was exclusively about money," Doc said. "I'm guessing here, Mark, but your blogs seem to indicate you do your research thoroughly.

I'm sure you know I'm not that popular with a few folks." I nodded. He chuckled.

"Does that bother you?" I asked. He laughed softly as I added, "Some of these people are ripping on you pretty hard."

"Small minds talk about people. Average minds talk about events. Great minds talk about ideas." He winked. "Let's talk about some ideas, Mark."

Chapter Eight

Insecurity, Defeat and Misfortune

kay. Let's talk about ideas", I said. "But, first, I'd be remiss if I didn't press you about your feelings. How do you feel about the negativity towards you that your competitors openly share throughout the Internet?"

What happened next changed my life. Check that. What happened next gave me the opportunity to change my life, to create a different outcome. I took it, once I really understood his three-word answer and, today, find myself living inside my dream, wealthy in unimaginable ways, because of it. And the wealth keeps growing.

"Just love them," Doc said emphatically. At the time I thought he'd expand, explain, do *something*. Nope, that was it, *Just love them.*

"But these are feelings. Let's stay with ideas, shall we?" he prompted. "All I can tell you is that if someone never moves out of a place of insecurity, they'll never understand defeat, nor what a great teacher defeat really is. If people can't understand defeat, they can never know the difference between defeat and misfortune. When we're stuck in the insecurity cycle, we are playing not to lose. Playing not to lose, hanging in there, competing, and measuring ourselves against others fosters fear. Playing not to lose has nothing to do with wealth and makes us singular in our perception of success. Usually money and the pie thing."

"What do you mean... the 'pie thing'?"

He explained that as long as people think that income is finite, they really believe that more for someone else means less for them. "For example, if I get a quarter of the pie, that only leaves three-fourths for everyone else."

"Oh, I see."

"You do?" Doc asked, with a soft chuckle and knowing eyes. After a pause, he added, "Yeah, I'm sure you see the metaphor, but maybe not the subtext of it. I sure didn't get the deeper meaning, which was another reason why Toni was reluctant to share the Ancient Verities of unilateral wealth, wealth in all areas of one's life."

"Verities?" I asked.

More chuckling, and more head nodding ensued. "I had the same question. A verity is a true principle". Seemingly out of the blue, he said, "Before we go any further, you must give me your word you will use a pseudonym to write about the Seven Ancient Verities, if we decide to move forward with the *'sort of a book thing'*. Promise me you will change the names of everyone, too. The Seven Ancient Verities need to be the focus, not the author, and not the people, and, most of all, not the wealth".

He paused, studying my face. "After all," he continued, "The Verities date back over 4,000 years. It all comes down to a choice between the ego for short-term fame and being in service anonymously and, thus, becoming wealthy beyond your imagination," he paused, laughing deeply, from his belly, "Sounds kind of biblical when I say it out loud, doesn't it?" Then, his face relaxed, he leaned forward, looked me dead in the eye and said, "Ego and money, or wealth and peace of mind?"

"May I ask you, well, I'm saying wealth… but, may I ask you about the subtext thing? About the pie metaphor that you said you missed the subtext message, too?" I asked.

Doc leaned further forward, got a very serious look in his eyes, and said, "Are you in, or are you out?"

"I don't even know what I'm agreeing to do." I'm sure I sounded annoyed. "I'm going to tell you a story—my story—and, then, if you desire, I'll share the Seven Ancient Verities with you. You write it as you see fit, the

story that is. But do not alter the ancient truth principles—the verities— and write it under a pen name. There is, perhaps, a payoff bigger than being a well-known author. You'll learn exactly how to mine untold wealth in all areas of your life, how to put the verities into play effortlessly," he explained.

"Why hasn't this been written and shared before now?" I'm stalling.

"Ego or wealth… are you in, or are you out?" he asked again, leaning back and locking those blue-green eyes of his with mine.

I sat there, trying to figure out how to convince him to let me write the book under my own name, but the ring of truth can have a very compelling draw to it. Try as I might, I knew that ego—my ego—was at the core of all the racing to different rationalizations I was running in my mind. There it was: the choice. Ego or wealth? The eternal human drama, the one that you, yourself, will face in a few pages, as you discover the Seven Ancient Verities.

I quickly realized the key factor in this decision was trust. Did I trust what he was offering as choices, that I could acquire untold wealth? "In."

I heard the word escaping my mouth and froze.

Thunder did not boom and lightning did not strike. Yet this was the moment after which my life would never be the same. Somehow, I knew I was more than "in". I was "all in."

Insecurity

Doc grew up in a small, old mill town in Massachusetts. As a kid, Doc played a lot of sports, and, once he graduated college, he got a job selling insurance. Then books. Then insurance again. He sold pots and pans up and down the East Coast with what he refers to as a "crew" of peddlers. He shared that there was always a gnawing feeling within a feeling of uneasiness that came from constant measuring; comparing his performance against everyone else.

"Worse yet, what made the gnawing feeling so powerful was that I had no idea how wealthy I was. The pattern of living and dying with each game as a kid then each week's sales as a pitchman… thinking, somehow, that results determined my value as a person was something I reinforced over and over. It became a habit, and, let's face it, we are our habits." Doc's voice trailed off. "Really, I had no idea how wealthy I was. It happened in the blink of an eye; it really did. I had swapped myself for symbols, and that, my friend, is where all insecurity comes from."

I interrupted and questioned him about his statement that all insecurity comes from swapping ourselves, for what he called "our personal power", for symbols of power. Almost dismissively, he said it was detailed in the Third Verity.

Looking at his life over the next fifteen years after graduation, most people would have deemed him successful. However, below the surface, the "big three" kept tormenting him. Fear. Doubt. And insecurity.

"Sales was something I never really liked, yet I stuck with it. It's kind of like sports, I guess. That's why I kept doing it," he said.

"How is sales like sports, Doc?"

"It's competitive, and, just like a game, you never really know what the outcome is going to be. It's why people watch it so much; you just don't know who is going to win, lose… where the hero will come from," he explained.

Always a top producer, he had won awards from two huge insurance companies, as well as Britannica. He had won a trip to the Super Bowl and earned great paychecks but in spite of that, there were two things he shared that I found particularly fascinating. First, he never had a paycheck; he only got paid for what he sold that week. Secondly, every Monday morning for fifteen years or so, the "big three" were churning in his gut. Fear. Doubt. Insecurity.

"I used to tell people that I believed life was a commission, so you might as well have a commission job and get paid what you are worth. It was all bullshit. It was eating me up," he continued in a subdued voice, "and, while I sounded confident, my behavior was self-destructive. Every time I was offered management, I found ways to ramp up self-destructive behavior, to do something that would sabotage it, and find some reason to bail."

"Bail?"

"Quit."

"And the seafood business?" I asked him.

Defeat

Doc's next business venture was one in which he worked for himself. Selling and delivering seafood was good money, especially once he'd built a route of regular deliveries and steadier income. During this phase of his life, Doc said, that big knot of insecurity in his belly was still there, but not as large as it had been during his sales days. About seven years into that business, he met a girl and had a daughter, Cheyenne. He had a ten-year- old son, Giovanni, but the marriage to his mother ended because they were young and both self-destructive. Doc promised himself in 1986, the year his daughter was born, that he'd correct his self-destructive flaws. He'd be a better father to his daughter than he had been to his son. It was not a big deal Doc thought. He'd just promise to stop hurting himself, stop repeating the self-destructive behavior.

Failed. A few times. Miserably.

"I just loved that kid, so, after more misery, I surrendered. I laid down my ego, joined a group, and got well. I healed a day at a time," Doc recounted. When I asked him which group, he ignored the question and gave me the next few chapters of his story.

He tried five different home-based businesses after that. He was still making good money on the seafood route, so he said, "The five defeats in those attempts were no big deal."

"What kind of businesses were they?" I wasn't just asking to ask, I really was curious. At that point in his life, Doc had clearly been a competitive guy and everybody knows competitors don't like failing.

In essence, they were all the same. Network marketing companies, like NuSkin, Herbalife, and so forth. He worked them part-time at night, after working the seafood route. He had the time, because the relationship that yielded the daughter was over almost as quickly as it started. He was living alone.

Confident, competitive people don't usually dismiss losses or defeats, yet it seemed like he was nonchalant about one failed attempt after another. It didn't seem to fit the openness he'd displayed up to this point. So I pressed.

"I didn't care that much, because I was earning more than I needed hustling seafood, and I got my daughter every weekend, every single weekend. I was old enough and clear enough in my mind to know that, while second chances are wonderful, they do not come in unlimited quantities. This was a second chance to be a father, a dad. Not just a guy who earned money, but a guy who was really involved. I loved that kid and still do. It would have been just like me to start missing time with the important people in my life who I shut out so often when I was a mess." Doc paused, then said, "defeats suck, and those were five defeats. I'm not denying that. I can handle defeat, but screwing up relationships with selfish neglect is something else altogether."

We had talked quite a while about the relationships and business defeats, when it finally occurred to me that he just had a different set of values than any business person I ever met. He measured himself by those values. He had successes in sales by anyone's standards. Yet he was insecure. He ran from them. The failures, all five, try as I might, drew no emotion from him at all. What the hell was going on? I told him that I was confused and he just chuckled, again.

It's not that complicated, he explained. "Look, I failed, got my ass kicked in the same arena five times, and, while I didn't like it, I was winning the only thing that mattered. I was winning me."

"What does that mean?" It was not a new idea, this winning of oneself, but I really did want to know what it meant to Doc. He said that we were back to the swapping self for symbols, and that we'd cover it in the Seven Ancient Verities. I told him that I needed more, that we needed to "move off this cryptic stuff" and get to the real story.

He got very serious, leaned forward, peered right at me, and said, "You can never get there. Nope, you can't get there."

"Then, why am I here?" I asked. Doc shouted, "Exactly!"

"What? What the hell are you talking about?" I'm almost yelling. "There. You can never get there," he says.

"Then... why am I here... why am I here with you now?" I repeated myself twice.

"Exactly."

Silence. I was glaring, trying to communicate how frustrated I was.

He started to giggle, and, then, as though trying to stop himself from giggling, he starts shaking all over with laughter and finally loses it. He sounded like a steam-engine locomotive, quickly regaling into a contagious laugher.

"What's so funny?" I'm almost indignant, trying not to be infected with his joy.

Doc answered, "I hear my former self, my pre-Verity self, when I was questioning things and expressing confusion."

Finally, Doc composed himself and started talking about irony. He said that the irony of what just happened is where the riches of life are found, and, if I am able to figure out how to write about it coherently, we would help a lot of people learn to help themselves; help people to Stand Tall and become wealthy in all areas of life, "all thirteen riches."

"Why is it ironic?"

"Look, you can never get *there* because once you get *there* ... you are here. Happiness, health... real wealth is here, not there. I mean, it might seem like we're playing with words, but we are not. The Verities and the thirteen riches of life are *here*, not *there*. Most people believe life begins for them when they get someplace, ya know? When they get *there*. We all get trapped in that moving goal post thing. That's the irony! Trying to get *there* prevents us from being *here*, and *here* is the only place wealth can be."

I told him I was really confused with the "here and there" thing, as well as what he meant by getting trapped in "that moving goal post thing."

He asked me to walk across the lanai and pointed to a spot. "Go over there." I did as I was told. He disappeared through the sliders and asked me to yell my location to him. "So, tell me, if I was looking for you, would you say, 'I'm there', or would you say 'I'm here?'"

"I'm here."

He returned to the lanai. "I told you to go over *there*…but, when I asked you where you were, you said *I'm here*. You can never get *there*," Doc exclaimed. "As soon as you get *there*, you are *here*. Toni taught me that, just as she passed the Ancient Verities on to me, just as they had been passed on to her."

He moved towards me, smiling, but still carrying a sadness in his eyes that belied the smile. Doc gently touched my face with the tips of his fingers and tapped me lightly on my cheek a couple of times. His smile was gone. "It's right here, overwhelming wealth and wonder. People are virtually drowning in it, but they think it's *there*. They just don't know it's *here*, and, sadly, we miss it." We sat back down, and Doc was very quiet for a long time, looking pensive. Finally, he broke the silence, "That's why I want to do this *sort of book thing* and change that."

"And the goal posts?" I asked. *"Moving goal posts."* "What?"

Doc went on to explain that the moving goals posts idea is really a simple metaphor for the same thing as the "here-and-there" idea. If happiness, wealth, or peace of mind is on the other side of the goal post, and every time you get there, the goal posts are moved, we can never be happy, nor can we ever be wealthy. We can never have peace of mind. The "there" keeps changing, and, since we can only be *here* and never be *there,* moving the goal posts after each achievement results in a lifetime of trying to get someplace we never can be.

"Can you give me an example?"

"A kid goes to school and sets the goal of good grades. The kid gets good grades, so he can get into a good university. He graduates. Is he happy? Now, it is time for him to move his goal post again and get to get a good job. He celebrates for a day, but not really. He already has targets, goal posts, set around job performance. Then, he'll be happy and wealthy. He hits his performance targets, and, immediately, new criteria for achievement, promotion, whatever… is set. Actually preset. He hits the targets again, crosses the goal line, and *boom,* new targets." At this point, Doc became *really* animated. "We get bullied adroitly into this pattern at work, in relationships, and the goal becomes retirement…kids, marriage. It's always *there*, and, if the *there* keeps moving, wealth, the true riches of life, including money is never here. It's there."

Misfortune

The obvious question for me was, *What changed that for Doc? What really changes for anybody?*

29

"So, what triggered the change for you, and how did you start living your dream?"

"Misfortune, unfortunately. For most people, it's misfortune. It doesn't have to be, but that's the way it works most of the time. It sure was for me."

"How so?" I asked.

He told me that this misfortune thing was nothing new, and that he had first read about it when studying Napoleon Hill. In Hill's self-help classic *Think and Grow Rich*, he studied rags-to-riches people face-to-face for twenty-five years, at the end of which he postulated that "opportunity often comes disguised in misfortune or temporary defeat."

"And for you?"

"Misfortune. And in a cluster."

So that's the backstory... here's how misfortune led Doc to stumble into wealth beyond measure.

Doc's first ex-wife had moved back to Georgia with their son. He saw the kid over the holidays and for about seven weeks in the summer. This went on for several years. Doc was pleased with the arrangement outwardly, but his heart longed for the periods of months without seeing the boy to be different. His ex-wife just could not get away from her self-destructive addiction, booze. The son was everything to her, and it was truly a magnificent gesture when she gave up the daily care to Doc. He was moved and grateful for a second chance. He'd dealt with his own self-destructivebehavior a couple years earlier.

Bewildered at this unmerited gift to be a daily, hands-on dad reached a crescendo when he picked the boy up at the airport in Boston. Driving north towards Plum Island, he had a hard time keeping his eyes on the road. He kept looking over at the boy. It was only a few years earlier that Doc's life had been a disaster; an unmanageable train-wreck mired in addiction. It felt surreal. He had a hard time believing it was really true but it was true. The evidence was sitting right there in his delivery van.

Doc's seafood business and route he'd built was earning enough money to cover his weekly nut, and then some. Things were good. He had plans for things he and the boy could do that were not a financial stretch.

He was still on an emotional high the following morning, when he headed to the wholesaler in Boston. Teddy, the salesperson at the wholesaler where he picked up his seafood, had some bad news. The seafood industry was about to undergo a major change. His company was going to move into compliance six months early, while others fought the unwinnable fight. Teddy, who'd earned Doc's trust, told him that people and companies that got into compliance with the new rules about handling seafood would benefit later, as hangers-on to the old way got closed up.

They sat and talked. The bucks to get into compliance—to get the kind of truck and equipment required—were a fairytale. Not only did Doc not have the $50,000 or so it would take, he did not see how he'd ever really recover it, since the price of fish was going to jump dramatically. It didn't take complicated spreadsheets and analysis for Doc to figure out his income was going to drop by 25 percent—quickly.

Then, things got worse.

Teddy told Doc that the company was not going to extend credit lines to cover the increase in pricing. Less inventory, and higher prices now brought Doc's loss of income over the coming six months closer to 50 percent. Less profit coming in than expenses to live was not a threat, it was a reality that happened in the blink of an eye. Suddenly, the celebrated second chance as a Dad, free from addiction, took an entirely different emotional pathway. Doc remembered thinking. "first pass for the kid was seeing me mostly as absent clown in his life and now he was going to see me fail." Terror hit.

Then, things got worse.

The bright, blue-eyed boy had been waiting for his dad to get home, and he came out to greet Doc as the delivery van pulled into the driveway. He was smiling. Doc pasted a smile on and yelled out the window, "Let's head up to the high school and get you registered!"

"Nana called, Dad," the boy said, "she called five times."

Nana, Doc's mother, was a very active woman who had been told by her physician that he would have to let the state know that she was no longer able to drive. Her glaucoma was progressing, and she would be legally blind within a few months. The seven-year battle for her eyesight had come to its inevitable conclusion. There was no consoling her, even with assurances from Doc that he would be her permanent caretaker. A prideful, self-reliant woman found that more depressing than reassuring. Her biggest fear, like many of the elderly from the Last Great Generation, was being a burden, and, in her mind, her greatest fear was coming true.

Doc told her that he and the boy were on the way to her house, as soon as they stopped by the high school, and they'd work out support systems.

31

When Doc hung up, the boy told him, "You need to call Chris. She called three times."

Then, things got worse.

Chris was Cheyenne's mom. When the boy was released by his mother, Doc had held a hope, a dream that reconciliation with Chris would give him a chance at a family of four, living under one roof. He had thought about it daily, holding that vision. Chris had something else in mind. She told Doc she'd met someone who was going to fund her going to school full-time and wanted to have Doc take the daughter more than just on the weekends. The girl was nine or ten years younger than her brother and, clearly, would require more daily support than the boy.

Within this twenty-four hour period, Doc was taking a cut in pay, becoming the primary caretaker for his mother, and becoming a full-time parent. Not only that, the dream he'd held was obliterated.

He was glad the boy was watching him. Giving assurances to the boy prevented Doc from acting out on his panic. In recounting this 24-hour period to me, Doc told me that having his dream crushed wasn't all that bad, reconciliation with Chris was a disaster waiting to happen and would be a daily pride-swallowing siege. They just were not a match. He was actually excited about more time with his daughter and having both of his children under one roof, but he could not see how to handle the time and financial problems.

Two months later, the income loss was taking its toll. Doc's son was even using masking tape to hold his sneakers together. On his way to the electric company to pay the bill and to keep the lights on, Doc promised his son that they would get new sneakers that night. He was going to peddle some smaller bags of seafood after servicing what was left on his route. He hit a curb and blew out a tire.

Now, he has a choice. Fix the tire, keep his promise to his son, buy the sneakers and let the lights go off... or... fix the tire, pay the electric bill and break the promise to his son. It was not a positive mental attitude and determination Doc had been carrying, it was denial. It was misfortune, plain and simple.

That was mid-September of 1993. Doc was poor and desperation set in.

Chapter Nine

The Gift of Desperation

As Doc tells it, a guy named Sean Gurken who Doc had taught to sell Britannica 18 years earlier called him in January of 1993 with a home-based business opportunity. It was a multi-level marketing company, in which independent distributors sell products and persuade other people to join their team or "downline" by selling, too. Sean wanted Doc to join the new company. Doc had already failed in the industry five times, and Sean had been involved in three of the failures with him. Sean had been the one to enroll Doc into three of those network marketing businesses, left without telling Doc, and, then, tried to get people on Doc's team to join him in the "next big thing."

Needless to say, Doc and Sean's conversation was ugly. There were lots of four-letter words directed from Doc to Sean. Sean confessed that he'd had a gambling problem, had ended the addiction, and wanted to make it up to Doc. Doc told him he was glad to hear it, was rooting for Sean, and as an obsessive-compulsive person, himself, understood. "But... don't ever call me about business again!" Doc shouted. He told Sean that anything—kids, family, sports, addiction recovery, anything really—was okay to discuss, but not business, which he emphasized with several "fbombs."

Things change, always.

Doc got what he described as the gift of desperation, wherein pride takes a backseat to need. It was September of 1993, and the siege of misfortune had struck: Doc's income was plummeting, and he was raising the kids on his own. He decided to call Sean, half hoping he'd not done much and half hoping he was making great money and could provide a solution.

It was here that Doc went into great detail about most people not seeing that their misfortunes are just opportunities in disguise. He said that there was no reason for anyone to go through what he went through, and that pain was mandatory, but suffering was optional. He laughed about himself, confessing that Sean's name had popped into his head the moment Teddy had given him the bad news about changes in the seafood business. During next few months, a voice within him had whispered Sean's name over and over.

"So, why didn't you call him? Pride?" I asked. "No. Self-centeredness and denial," Doc replied.

Finally, Doc called Sean and was surprised to find out that he was making $1,800 a week. Doc did not believe him. Sean's history of exaggerating was plentiful. Doc demanded that Sean fax him copies of checks, and, when they arrived, Doc joined, borrowing most of the $400 to get started. Then, things got worse.

Doc was hustling seafood by day and working on the phone, making sales calls, at night. He was trying to get people to join a network marketing company called Market America. Doc was failing the same way he'd failed five times before. This time, though, he had the gift of desperation. He sat the kids down and told them that Dad would be working from seven to ten on the phone.

He felt bad about the fact that his son, Giovanni, had to be a sort of substitute parent to his sister. He felt bad about working 13, 14, and 15 hours a day, seven days a week. He felt bad, but he hoped and wanted to believe it would be temporary. He was able to maintain that drive for a while, but hope started slipping away as hopeless started pushing its way in. Doc was about to be behind on the rent—not making a business work is one thing, but not having shelter for the family is a whole different level of stress.

Doc heard about a well-known speaker who was going to be in Hartford, Connecticut and rolled the change from the "vacation" jar he and the kids had. He drove two hours to Hartford, stayed in the room for 15 minutes, and realized it was a waste of time. It was just another self-appointed expert who was preaching goals and persistence. Doc knew the guy was leading to an upsell that would be a rehash of all the run-of-the-mill self- help crap. He wandered into the hallway. He must have looked terrible, because a concerned looking stranger stopped at the sight of him.

"Man, are you okay?" he asked.

Doc broke down in tears and told the guy that he might not even have enough gas to get home… home to two kids he couldn't support, two failing businesses, and a blind mother. The stranger walked him over to a couch. As luck would have it, the stranger happened to be fairly successful in home-based businesses and shared one tip that gave Doc hope.

Things Get Better, Temporarily

The tips that the stranger shared were common sense. He told Doc that if he wanted to make some money, he'd have to acquire certain skills. He shared one of those skills with Doc, who tried it out the next day, and, to his surprise, it worked. Doc started earning $300 checks every week. It was not enough money to solve all his challenges, but it was hope, which he so desperately needed at the time.

Doc continued to grind the seafood route during the day and network marketing at night and on the weekends. He began to attend training events, all-day "Super Saturday" events that the company held every six weeks or so. Within a year, Doc was earning about $5,000 a month through network marketing, and his achievements were recognized on stage. "At that point," he said, "things were looking up."

Chapter Ten

Toni, Peter and Bill

One Friday night, Doc received a call from the gal organizing the upcoming "Super Saturday" seminar. She told him that, instead of just asking him to take a bow for his achievements, they would also want him to spend 15 minutes sharing how he was getting results and growing. Excited, Doc began composing and practicing his speech.

Toni and Peter, a couple from Hartford, Connecticut, by way of Houston, who were earning over $25,000 per month, were the featured speakers for that seminar. They were incredibly vibrant and informative. And more. There was something familiar about them, but Doc just could not put his finger on it.

Try as he may to study his notes for his speaking part after the lunch break, he was fascinated, almost obsessed, with how he knew Toni and Peter. By 10:30 AM, he had completely forgotten that he was speaking and dialed into Toni, who was doing most of the sharing from stage with the audience of just over 300 people. He kept asking himself, *Why does she seem so familiar? Did I meet her and her husband on one of my trips to Houston while visiting my brother?*

"It kept running through my head... how do I know her... how do I know her..." he recounted, adding with a wink, "I'm a tad obsessive fromtime to time."

Toni was explaining how to recruit people to look at the business, and Doc heard her use the word *acceptance* a couple of times. What was significant to Doc about the training was hearing the word *acceptance* used several times in regard to rejection, along with the phrases *clean house and help others*. At that point, Doc's curiosity began to turn into a hunch.

All of the speakers ate lunch together with the organizers of the seminar, and, since Doc was one of the speakers, he was invited. He listened intently as the affable couple conversed during the meal. Doc's eyes flitted back and forth from Toni to Peter. Toni uttered the phrase, *live and let live* a second time, piquing Doc's investigative mind. The gal directing the event said that they were going to do the recognition right after the lunch break, culminating with Doc, who had just gotten to the $5,000 per month milestone.

They congratulated Doc, and he asked if they needed to know what he was sharing, so he wouldn't steal their thunder. Toni smiled, assuring Doc not to worry about it. She advised him to be himself and to relax

"Just take it one minute at a time up there," she said, with a comforting smile. At that point, there was no doubt in Doc's mind what the connection he kept feeling was.

As they broke from lunch, Toni and Peter were still being asked questions. Everyone wanted to know how the couple got to $25,000 a month. Peter broke it off, telling everyone they need to head up to their room to prepare for the afternoon session. Doc was watching all of this and merged with them as they left the restaurant and headed to the elevators.

In one of the hallways of the hotel, he asked for permission for a non-business question, and, despite Peter's assertion that they really needed to get to the room, Toni engaged.

"Do you know Bill?" Doc asked, almost a whisper. Toni and Peter stopped, looked at each other, smiled, and looked back at Doc.

"We've known Bill for seven years; Peter's known him for six years. You?"

"Seven."

At this point in the story, I asked Doc what this was all about, this Bill guy. He continued with the story, ignoring my question completely.

"Who's Bill?" I pressed.

Doc explained that he couldn't really say, because the traditions of this quasi-clandestine subculture are opposed to any publicity or press at any level. He told me that it's where he went to surrender from his self-destructive behavior. "It's a group that helps people help themselves replace self-destructive behavior with a spiritual life."

"Are you talking about Alcoholics Anonymous?" I surmised.

Doc replied, "Let just leave it at this. I used to drink, now I don't. The answer to your next question is 28 years."

Toni, Peter, and Doc's discovery of their mutual friend Bill stopped all three of them in their tracks. Hugs followed. *Real* ones.

They asked Doc if he was coming to dinner after the seminar with the other leaders. He explained he had declined, so that he could get home to his children, but, since the boy was older, he might be able to return later in the evening, if they would like. They told him that they wanted him to return, so he did.

Doc spoke with Toni and Peter in their hotel room for hours. They talked about their common bond, the suffering they'd inflicted upon themselves, and the subsequent recovery.

When he finally left sometime around two or three in the morning, they all knew that it was the beginning of a beautiful friendship.

Chapter Eleven

Treasure Hunting and Treasured

oc didn't share very much about the conversation he, Toni, and Peter had had until the wee hours of the morning. He said I'd have to be content with his general description... "anonymity, and all that," he explained. He gushed about the intimacy, how the common suffering prior to meeting "Bill" creates a no bullshit bond that's virtually instant.

Over the next year, there was about a conversation a month between Doc and the couple. Toni treasured the friendship, the bond between her and Doc. Evidently, when couples get sober, they become different people and believe they have to learn how to relate to each other in new ways. Doc was helpful in her quest, getting her to see it as an adventure, a new experience. As her relationship with Peter moved forward and beyond what she had hoped for initially, the relationship with Doc became even more treasured.

On the other hand, Doc was seeking the treasure. He wanted to know how to break through from decent earnings to the kind of bucks Toni and Peter were earning. That brings us back to the opening of this story, when Toni declined to share what she had discovered; how it was that the couple's income was now over $36,000 every month and how they had such peace of mind about all of it.

Doc kept moving forward with the idea that their income had yielded the security that led to the peace of mind Toni and Peter exhibited and he wanted. They spoke at least once a month, usually with all three of them. They talked about Bill, business, relationships, the whole gambit of topics that good friends usually talk about. Over the course of the next year, Doc came to understand why Toni was reluctant to give him what he asked for each time they spoke. He didn't like it, but, thankfully, he had no longer had any resentment about it.

As Doc can best recall, around five or six months into their friendship, things started changing. One night was very different. Their call started with the same initial dialog, but, on this particular occasion, Toni opened up and laid out her reason for holding back about how they experienced such great business growth.

"Once I share this with you, it will change everything between the three of us. It will require a daily commitment, and, if you don't keep the commitment when we see one another or chat on the phone, it will be different. While money is great, the real treasure in life is finding people you can be yourself with, totally open with...and they love you, anyway. We, all three of us, feel safe to be ourselves...crazy, angry, whatever. I've been squirrely at times, and I never get off the phone feeling like I must have sounded like a nut or that you think worse of me," Toni explained, pausing. She continued, "I know you love us both, and we love you. I know if I give this to you, and you don't do it, exactly as it's laid out, it will alter our relationship. I'm not willing to risk that greatest of all treasures just yet. Until you understand, in your heart, that security issues are all fear-based, the message of what I want to give you won't land in your heart. Unless it lands in your heart, you won't complete it, and that will divide us in ways I refuse to even think about."

Doc pitched hard for her to change her mind. He realized that he did not really understand the security thing, that all efforts to create security were fear-based. When he tried to ask her to explain the security thing, he interrupted himself, laughing, "You're just going to tell me I've got to figure that out myself, right?" he guessed. Toni giggled and assured Doc that it was not a test. She'd know, he'd know, and their mutual treasure would continue to grow.

Things Get Worse

Doc kept treasure-hunting, trying to drive income beyond what he needed to support the kids and himself and felt frustrated because it just was not happening. Two credit cards showed up with $10,000 lines of credit about a week before the engine in the van he delivered seafood in seized up. Doc made a decision to go for it all and used the checks that came with the credit cards to give himself $20,000 in cash advances.

He leased an Infiniti J30, figuring that he had about seven or eight months to get his income over $10,000 a month, pay back the debt, and be on his way to what Toni and Peter were earning. After all, he thought, doing the network marketing business full-time, instead of part-time, would give him more time with the kids and give the business a real chance to earn money. Doc's reasoning was clear to him when writing out those cash advances, *If I'm not willing to invest in myself, why would others invest in me?*

Two months later, his income hadn't budged. The positive feeling he had about being worth investing in himself, instead of buying another beat-up van, had morphed into stress. During that time, sad and mad were the two

40

moods that featured prominently in Doc's life, often rapidly shifting from one to the other and back again. Regret was there, too. It was hard work not pushing Toni when they talked, and he told her that. She said she loved that he was sharing how he felt and to keep thinking about the idea that all searches for security were fear-based. Most of the feelings he had had years earlier, when he was in direct sales, were resurfacing.

Doc was reading classic self-help books, like Napoleon Hill's *Think and Grow Rich* and Og Mandino's *The Greatest Salesman in the World,* and he was going back to his early training materials provided by the great billionaire and insurance mogul W. Clement Stone. Three months later, his income was inching up, but it wasn't fast enough. In four or five more months, he would be out of money, out of credit, and, worst of all, out of house. He was certain there was something in the books that he was missing.

He mastered the success formula from *Think and Grow Rich;* he almost knew the book by heart, yet growing rich was just was not happening. The question, *What am I doing wrong?,* plagued him to the point of obsession. Still, he stuck with it, hoping that he would soon discover what he was missing.

Instead, he encountered more anger, more sadness, and more regret. Worse still was that he was not crazy about the person he was right at that moment.

"When I was going through this," Doc recounted, "watching financial disaster moving closer, I was full of fear. I was obsessive and impatient. I kept working harder and spending less time with the kids. I was working so much and hoping that my constant impatience and fear wouldn't spill over on them. I wasn't successful at that, either. It really sucks when you're short-tempered and snapping at people, snapping at your kids, when you are trying to make them feel safe and valued."

A Storm and Birds

Plum Island is a nine-mile-long sliver of a land mass just off the northern coast of Massachusetts. There are lots of "Nor'easter" storms during the winter. One night, a doozy rolled in, bringing with it snow, thunder, lighting braking a couple branches off some of the trees in the backyard. ·

The next morning, Doc headed out the back porch with his coffee and some birdseed as usual. He noticed some broken branches scattered around the backyard. It was early and quiet. The kids weren't awake yet. Plum Island is a bird sanctuary, and, even though many had gone south for the winter, many species remained. In the quiet, Doc began thinking about what Toni meant when she said that trying to get things that will make him feel more secure is fear-based.

He noticed some of birds were landing on the broken branches and his heart began to race. As he tells the story, he immediately ran to call Toni. He believed that he had figured out what he needed to know for her to finally share her discovery with him.

He called Toni, but the call went to her answering machine. Doc headed back to the porch and left the door open, so he could hear the phone when she called back. He kept watching the birds land on the branches, flit over to the bowl of birdseed, and flit back to a branch, Doc's heart beating faster. Finally, the phone rings. It's Toni.

Recounting the story, Doc says that when he told Toni what he saw, he heard her yell Peter's name two or three times, "really more of a shriek." Peter joined Doc and Toni on the other phone, and Toni had Doc tell Peter what he just shared with her. At that point, she was weeping.

"Trust. The birds don't worry about where they land; they trust their wings, not the branch. They trust their gift," Doc said.

"More," shouted Peter, extolling Doc.

There is a long, long silence. Doc was thinking.

"I believed that when I reach a certain income level, I'll be safe and secure, calmer and that, because of that, I would be a better person and a better dad … It's an illusion, a lie," Doc said, on a roll. "Nothing outside of me can ever make me feel secure, until I trust myself. Security from things, money, and recognition is a falsehood that it seems like everyone is chasing… that I have been chasing."

Toni's weeping had turned to sobs, and the three friends talked for hours.

42

Chapter Twelve

The Seven Ancient Verities

Toni was having a difficult time shutting down the tears. She told Doc—between sniffles and outbursts—that there are Seven Ancient Verities that pave the way for the 13 Riches of Life. She called it Standing Tall. Learning the Verities and mastering them helps one Stand Tall and claim the 13 Riches of Life. She and Peter had held them for years, she said, but the total of their riches would only be a fraction of their value to them, until they passed the Ancient Verities to a worthy recipient. Toni told Doc that the responsibility of finding the right person to pass them onto had been a burden of sorts.

"A burden?" Doc was puzzled.

Peter explained that the debt of gratitude they have, everything they have, which all came from the Verities, began to weigh on them about five years ago. They'd been in possession of them for over ten years at that point and began to realize that the final responsibility they had agreed to when they were given the Ancient Verities was to pass them on to someone who would ensure they were passed on intact. And they had also agreed to something bigger with their promise "pass along" the Verities. That "something bigger" increased the burden.

Doc tried to joke, asking if he'd be entering some clandestine culture and signing over his soul. He asked if there was some kind of secret handshake or covenant sealed in blood. They both ignored Doc's attempts at humor.

Peter, stepping in for the still sniffling Toni, told Doc, "Should you decide to embrace these Seven Ancient Verities exactly as prescribed, you will find yourself in the great adventure; actually, the greatest of all adventures. Self-discovery. Within that adventure, you'll acquire all 13 riches life has to offer." Peter was very somber as he explained that there was a "but," and his voice trailed off. A loud, long silence hung over the phone line.

"There are," Toni explained, "requirements and a huge responsibility that go along with accepting the Verities and the Map. I need to know that you understand the difference between getting relief from your current challenges and acquiring wealth... that wanting a solution to current conditions is not enough. You need to assure us that you aren't interested in improving your lot in life, but, instead, in growing this life—your life—in a different direction."

More silence. Doc was thinking.

"Peace of mind", he finally said. "If you're telling me that … I mean, if you're asking me if I've had enough of that gnawing feeling within my gut and want it extinguished, yeah, I'm about that."

"How do you really feel?"

"The loneliness, the feelings of never being enough... feelings of unworthiness and fear... an almost constant worry about the future. It's all so exhausting. There is this paradox—I want to do better; I act determined, yet I live with doubt makes me feel like a phony, ya know? Acting brave but being scared. I often wonder if I am the only person who feels that conflict, that phoniness between bravado and doubt... and, when I feel that conflict, I feel unbelievable loneliness... see what I'm saying, Toni?"

"I used to feel that way before we got the Ancient Verities and The Map," Toni replied.

"The Map?" Doc was intrigued, "Did you mention the map before? So, there are the Ancient Verities and a map?"

Peter jumped in, "Most people want The Map that leads to the 13 riches of life, and that's a mistake. See, navigating the road to wealth, focusing on wealth as the person we currently are, the person you currently are, Doc, will end in frustration, judgment, and failure to obtain the riches."

"I don't really understand. I love you, man, but, sometimes, you can be a little cryptic. Toni, could you please break it down for me?"

"It's this way, Doc," Toni explained. "The Map to the 13 Riches is what everybody thinks they want, but it's really of little to no value until we know how to read The Map. Most people are looking in the wrong place for the real treasures in life. Hell, we've shared three, four, five of the riches of life with people in conversation, and they just don't get it. They only want to know about the money, which—dating back over 4,500 years—is the last of the riches to be added."

"So... you're saying that the Map is of no value, until I learn how to read the Map? And to do that, I need to become a different person?"

"Not exactly," Peter corrected. "Let me tell you a story, a true story, one you'll read in the Verities, but it answers your question. Consider it a teaser. It seems that there was a party of sailors who were shipwrecked and drifting in the Atlantic Ocean in an open rescue boat. They'd been drifting for several days, had run out of water, and were starting to suffer the agonies of thirst. They had no water to drink. It was scary and frustrating... 'water, water everywhere but not a drop to drink,' as Coleridge once wrote."

"Let me tell the rest of it, Peter," Toni interrupted. "I just love this part. A couple of days of this, and, finally, another small boat came within hailing distance. Our shipwrecked mariners cried out for water, begging for water. The new sailors on the scene yelled back, "Let down your bucket." How cruel this must have sounded. They kept screaming for water, after two days of thirst. But all they got back several times was the phrase "let down your bucket".

"In desperation, one of the sailors threw the bucket overboard and pulled it back up. It was clean, fresh, sparkling water. For several days, these shipwrecked mariners had been drifting through fresh water and didn't know it. Yes, they were out of sight of land, but off the estuary of the Amazon, which carries fresh water many miles out to sea."

"Great story, Toni. Be okay if you explained what you want me to draw out of it, what the metaphor is?" Doc asked.

"You are surrounded by riches right now. The truth is the thirsty sailors were in fresh water all that time, they just did not know it. All you are really thirsting for, all the things most people are thirsting for, are already surrounding them, but, like the sailors, they don't know it. To acquire the 13 Riches of Life, two things are required. Just two things."

"And those two things are...?"

"The art of recognition and the act of recognition."

"I'm not real clear on what you are sharing. I just don't want to kind of know what you mean."

"The sailors did not recognize that they were sitting in fresh water. Once they learned they were, recognition alone was not enough, they needed to act on it." Toni continued, "We are rich right now. You have untold wealth surrounding you; you are sitting in it, you just don't know it. Unfortunately, this is the story of most people's lives. We have no idea, really, of immense number of resources and incredible tools within us, nor the riches we are all almost drowning in. This is why The Map to riches is of no value, until you learn how to throw down your bucket, Doc. So the Ancient Verities help you recognize the greatness that lives within you... in your character, not in your skills nor talents. Character. It is the character that matters. It is the character of a person that makes

45

understanding and following the map to unimaginable wealth easy, virtually effortless. Without character, we just don't see the riches. Without character, we don't recognize them. And we can't act on things we don't recognize."

"Greatness?"

"There are no common people, Doc, just great people who have been conditioned to behave commonly, to follow the herd, to value things, instead of themselves."

"Greatness?" Doc asked, perplexed.

"Character is what makes us great. Have you ever said he's a great guy or she's a great person?" Toni asked.

Toni's voice got very soft, quiet to the point that Doc could hardly hear her. "The world has fame and greatness and values all mixed up. Those people you think are great are great because…?"

Doc began beating around the bush, "Well, that depends on…" She interrupted Doc, empathically restating her question, "Who? Tell me who, right off the top of your head, you think is great."

"My uncles Dan and Mo."

"Tell me what makes them great, not what they have done for you, nor fond memories, but tell me what makes them great. Tell me about them and why you believe they are great."

Doc spoke for about a minute, recounting to her how his father had been killed in the Korean War, and Dan and Mo stepped in and beautifully filled the role of his father. "It was like I had two great dads, always there for me for everything, from playing baseball, to the difference between right and wrong and… " Toni interrupted him again.

"Do you know that you are describing their character and not their accomplishments?" she asked. "And they've enriched you and your life, Doc?"

"For sure."

"No person can enrich another's life if they do not have riches to share. We simply cannot give away what we do not have, and we cannot acquire any real wealth, we cannot grow wealth, until we give it away. The more we enrich others, the wealthier we become," she whispered.

Doc said, "That sounds great, but it's a little deep for me. Give me the child's version, okay?"

"The real wealth, the 13 Riches, are already within you. Like all of us, you've been conditioned to think it's something outside yourself that will make you wealthy. As long as we believe something external will make us feel safe, wealthy, secure... whatever feeling it is that we are searching for, we'll never develop the character within needed to be great and obtain the riches then share them. It is character—who you really are— that ignites the two things dormant within you to read The Map: the art of recognition and the act of recognition."

Doc asked the obvious question... if those were the only requirements.

"No, Doc, there is the big one, and that is sacrifice," Peter said.

Doc followed up with another obvious question, "What is the sacrifice?" "You. To truly grow, you have to be willing at any moment to sacrifice what you are for what you were intended to be... willing to give up your current self for the great character that is already within you." Toni explained. "Understand?"

Doc was quiet for several minutes. "Let me ask you this," Doc said. "I have to 'be' something different, so I will see things differently and do things differently, so I can have different things. Right?"

Toni and Peter simultaneously responded, "Yes."

"How do I do that—be something different—and still feel authentic?"

Doc broke away from the tale, looked at me, grinning, and winked. He pulled a piece of paper out of a folder and handed it to me. It was a copy of the email I sent to him a month before... the last paragraph was highlighted and circled.

Dear Doc

Your last email was difficult to understand, very wordy.

I'm not sure what the next step is, but, after spending some time on your site, I believe I know what my readers need to know to be more successful.

It's the be-do-have part, right?

> *One has to 'be' a different person so they can do different things which will let them have different things," seems to be the essence of what you are sharing. So I'm going to ask you, "how do we 'be' a different person yet retain who we really are? Not feel like we're imitating someone else?"*

47

It's not "What did you do to get what you got?" That's the wrong question.

Sincerely,

Mark

When I finished reading and looked up, Doc was still grinning. His eyes were misting up, and he winked at me again.

Chapter Thirteen

The Promise, The Pass, and The Bomb

As Doc tells it, he suddenly began firing questions at both Peter and Toni at remarkable pace, rattling them off without waiting for answers, piling one question on top of another. He wanted to know all about these Ancient Verities and the Map to the 13 Riches, and, quite candidly, so did I as I heard about them for the first time.

Peter made no attempt to answer any of them. Neither did Toni. "You

need to promise something first," said Toni.

"I can make the promises, but I need some answers before I do," Doc said. He still had a million unanswered questions and continued asking them... "Where did these Verities come from? How did you get them? Who wrote them?..."

"No, that's not going to work," said Peter countered.

"All the answers are in the Seven Verities, and so are the promises", Toni said.

"So what are these promises?" Doc asked.

"The passing of the Seven Verities is contingent on you promising to keep promises that you make. Are you willing to make this promise?"

"Yes."

"It's great that you have a lot of questions." Doc asked, "And that's great because…?"

Toni and Peter laughed. Managing a smile, himself, Doc said, "Yeah, I get it now, everything I ask is in these verities, right? One question…just one. It's a minor thing, just something you said that I wanted clarification on, that I heard it right."

"Okay."

"When you said these things, the verities, are 4,500 years old, was that an exaggeration? I mean 4,500 years? Really?"

"Let's meet out in Worcester, just off route 291, at that Italian place tonight," Toni suggested. "We'll have the Seven Verities with us, and The Map. They are handwritten; it took me a few hours. The passer of the Verities and Map have always done it by hand. You think about one thing on the way down. Think about making a promise to both of us that you will think before making promises and promise to keep the ones you make, no matter what."

"7:00?" Doc asked. "And the 4,500 year old thing, true?" "True." "How

can that be?" he asked, baffled.

"See you at 7:00, Doc."

The Promise

The trio had no sooner sat down at Piccolo's, the restaurant loved by all, when Toni asked Doc if he'd keep his promise when driving down and had an answer.

"Yeah, Toni, I'm in. Doc is here, Doc is all in." "Not the right words. Try it again," Toni said.

Doc was catching on, looked down, took a deep breath and made solid eye contact with Toni. "I promise that I will keep my promises, all of them." He turned to Peter and repeated himself.

The Pass

Toni passed the Seven Ancient Verities to Doc. "It's been over 4,500 years since these Verities were first recorded, and, now, it's your time to Stand Tall and acquire the 13 riches of life. Here are the instructions. Verities first—only the verities—and, then, The Map... You must Stand Tall, first, so you can see the real wealth on The Map."

Doc leaned forward, eager for more. There was no more. "Is that it? That's all the instructions?" Doc asked, somewhat mystified.

"That's it," Peter said. "By the way, do you like giraffes?"

"Yeah, I like giraffes... I'd say they're my favorite. Why do you ask?"

"Just wondering," said replied. "There is one more thing."

The Bomb

Speaking very quietly, Toni said, "Over the centuries, some of the language and stories got updated, but the Verities and Map remain the same at the core. Truth is truth, so to speak. At the turn of each millennium, the passer, that would be you, decides to pass it to one person, like we are doing with you, or give it to someone who brings it to the world."

"And you're telling me this because?"

"One of the people who these Verities pass through, the one who passed them to us, believes that love is in need of love, today, now," Peter chimed in. "We both agree."

"Yeah," Toni assented, "Love's in need of love today."

"Isn't love, real love, unconditional?" Doc asked, rhetorically.

"Well, that's what you get to figure out, Doc," Toni said. "You decide if love needs love, needs to be demonstrated more often, and how you complete the next pass," Toni said.

"I'm still wondering what this has to do with me…" Doc's voice faded, trailing off.

"The era of single passes needs to be over," Toni said forcefully, grabbing Doc's hand. "Bring it to the world, my dear friend. It's time."

Stunned, Doc asked who said love's in need of love today… knowing he'd probably be ignored.

"The directions and corresponding promises are in each Verity," Peter promised. "Just follow the directions, and keep the promise each Verity asks for. When you finish the Seven Verities as directed, let's meet here, eat more pasta, and we'll share what we know about some of the passes, who has had these Verities, and how they came to wealth."

"When are we going to do this?" Doc asked. "Fourteen weeks," Toni said.

"How do you know it's fourteen weeks?"

"Bring it to the world, Doc," Peter urged.

"And this is why you are here," Toni said, eyeing Doc with grace and hope. "We're hoping you will be the one who will bring The Verities and The Map to the world."

And that is a little more of the story of how this "sort of book thing" came to be, how it has come to your hands. Doc's unilateral wealth and mine too for that matter, and how we both came to understand why one must Stand Tall in character to see the Riches on The Map. It only happens through experiencing it. Once one learns to Stand Tall, meaning once one develops a deep understanding of the truth of being, their character stands out, Stands Tall, and with The Map, it becomes effortless to acquire all 13 riches.

I pass on to you the same words that Doc passed on to me, words I heeded, despite temptation, curiosity, and economic stress to go right to The Map. Doc said, "I encourage you to make the choice of the truly wealthy. Read each Verity as directed, and resist jumping to The Map of the 13 Riches until you, too, Stand Tall by making and keeping promises that grow your already fine character. Let it grow into the great force it was always intended to be. I promise that if you do, you will discover unilateral wealth. Real wealth always follows growth of character, and know this; there is no limit to your character."

When I received those instructions from Doc that I am passing to you, I had the same reaction you are probably having right now; "What? That's it? Aren't there any other instructions?" It's a funny thing about us humans. We ramble through life, certain that there must be a better way to be living, a better way to make a living, and, then, bam, someone says "here you go", our hopes and prayers suddenly answered, yet we resist, want more, want assurances, want guarantees, want someone to hold our hand, while, at the same time, coveting independence. And, for the most part, we don't want to follow the directions. Yup, we're an odd lot, us humans.

"Let's have dinner in fourteen weeks," Doc said.

"What's with this fourteen-week thing?" I probed, somewhat demandingly. The fear about what to do, exactly, was back and running at full throttle.

"Read each Verity as it is laid out, Mark, and I'll see you in fourteen weeks," he dismissed my question.

"Are you telling me that is all I need to know?" I asked. I had no idea what had just been handed to me, not the value of it anyway. "How about San Francisco?" Doc suggested.

"Okay," I said. Looking down at what he had handed me, I asked him, "Is this your handwriting?"

"Yes. Just follow the directions in each verity, and let yourself grow," he urged.

The Seven Ancient Verities

Look to this day! For it is life, the

very life of life, In its brief course

Lie all the verities and realities

of your existence:

The bliss of growth, The glory of action,

The splendor of beauty, For yesterday

is but a dream And tomorrow only a vision,

But today well lived makes every

yesterday a dream of happiness

And every tomorrow a vision of hope.

Look well, therefore, to this day!

Such is the salutation of the dawn.

Kalidasa 2500 BC Sanskrit

When wealth is lost, nothing is lost When

health is lost, something is lost

When character is lost, all is lost

The Promise

Within each being lives immense strength of character

If you resist the temptation of The Map's
Riches until you complete the Verities

Your character will grow taller than a giraffe and enable you
to see and claim the riches

And like the giraffe, which has the largest of all hearts, the verities
will grow your heart

Giving you courage, love and grace

These three character traits are all you need
to acquire the 13 Riches effortlessly

This is the flawless promise of the Verities

The First Verity

"The G"

Gratefully Give To The Dreams of Others and Grow Greatness

I am grateful that I am, day-by-day, minute-by-minute more and more aware of the infinite bounty surrounding me. Each passing moment I become more humbled by the unmerited gifts and opportunities continuously cascading into my life. Any shame my mind begins to experience for the self-centeredness I previously lived with and self-pity that blinded me from seeing the real riches of life I've always been blessed with is quickly extinguished by a great truth.

Now. Now is all there is. *Now* is all there ever was and *now* is all there ever will be. Everything that happened in the past happened when it was *now*. Same is true of the future. What happens two weeks from today can only happen two weeks from today. Whatever happens can only happen in the *now*. I am grateful for this truth and living in the *now* honors that truth within me.

I neither regret the past nor wish to close the door on it. Living in a state of gratitude right *now* is the vitalizing redemption from my self-centered perspective of lack. I use the past and my recollection of any selfishness that stole gratitude and riches from myself and others to appreciate the *now* should my mind wander into old thought habits of lack, entitlement or fear. I am present. I am grateful.

Since the beginning, century after century, all the illuminated minds have agreed and carried the same message about successfully acquiring wealth in all areas of life. Success is a result of service given without expectation of reciprocity.

Just as the stars can only reveal themselves after the sky darkens, so to my success can only appear after I am in service. The darker the sky, the more abundant and brighter the stars appear. *Now* I truly understand the greater my grateful giving is, the more abundant and brighter my prosperity shines.

I am a grateful giver and humble receiver.

The great verity, Gratefully Giving to the lives and dreams of others, is alive within me already. I need not work to have it yet I must open my mind to learn all of the wisdom this great verity carries so I may activate this unmerited gift currently dormant within me. All the other verities and The Map to the 13 Riches are contingent on the Verity of Giving and I am grateful that I understand its significance. Giving from my heart and without expectation helps me fathom the unfathomable; that which I share will multiply and return ten-fold while that which I hold will diminish.

The more I give, the more I shall receive.

Like all irrefutable laws, it works both ways. Give more, get more. Give more love, get more love. Give more kindness, get more kindness. Give more fear, doubt and lack to myself in thought or to others, the more fear, doubt and lack will grow in my life.

I am prepared to receive the greatest of all laws of the mind, the **Law of Growth.** What I think about grows. For all things, which are held in thought and charged with feeling, will grow and those things will become all of what I can give. I therefore focus on only those things I wish to receive like faith, hope and love.

I am a grateful giver and humble receiver.

Our true nature is to be of service to our fellow men and women. Being loyal to my true, service-driven nature grows my character, allowing me to Stand Tall, find and claim unilateral affluence with all life's meaningful currencies. Affluence comes from the word "afflure" meaning, "to flow to". Currency has its root in the word "currere" which means "to run".

All 13 great currencies, found on The Map, health, a positive mental attitude, purpose, money and 9 others are vibrant currencies. These currencies have value only when they flow, being constantly exchanged. How do I get them "to flow to" me? How does one become affluent? This is the mystery of the ages, perplexing and discouraging men and women for centuries. In my hands I now hold the First Verity which solves that mystery; *Giving is the fountainhead of incomprehensible affluence… not getting.* While others try to "get" affluence, I give it. I am grateful to know I must give to receive.

Yet no one can give what he or she does not have. What if I have none of the 13 riches to give? For those who know the First Verity and live in the *now*, this ancient enigma is simple to solve.

Gratitude is a cause, not an effect.

The greater my gratitude, the more things to be grateful for begin to flow into my life. Each gratitude flowing from my heart triggers even more things to be grateful for. They flow to me from a matrix of people, places and things, rarely from the channels I give to. I vow to be a better observer, taking nothing for granted... simple things like food, water and shelter make my heart joyful. I *now* give thanks in everything and become a humble receiver. The words "thank you" are said with sincere feeling constantly during the day. Sometimes I say "thank you" enthusiastically to a person, sometimes to a group and sometimes simply looking skyward.

I am a grateful giver and humble receiver.

I *now* know deeper wisdom of the Grateful Giving Verity. Giving without expectation of reciprocity is humbly honoring the Source of All Good. Each day brings a deeper understanding that I am both a channel and representative of The Source! Through the centuries those who have mastered the verities and acquired great wealth have always understood that this Source seeks the channels whereby it can render the greatest good, the most service for the greatest number of people. I love being a great channel for the Source of All Good and gratefully give all good that comes my way for I *now* know the greatest wisdom of the Giving Verity; *Seeds held are of no value. Seeds planted quickly become a forest.* I Stand Tall in character, plant seeds by giving and the 13 riches grow as a forest around me.

And when do I Stand Tall?

I begin *now*. All my choices are made by my subconscious mind; on this there is no debate. This means the life I have is the life I've chosen. It was not one big decision but a lifetime of weekly, daily and often minute-to-minute decisions. All the decisions are based on what my subconscious believes. I have therefore created all the circumstances in my life. This is wonderful news because it means I am creative! To make different decisions, create and acquire true wealth I must influence my subconscious mind so the decisions are different... thereby creating different actions and different, desirable results. I Stand Tall by building character *now*.

And how is this done?

Using the Law of Growth. A thought, charged with feeling becomes an idea in the subconscious. With repetition and feeling the subconscious will accept this new thought thus creating a new belief. My actions always become obedient to my beliefs. I follow the recipe of the Seven Ancient Verities exactly for I know making a cake with only half the ingredients yields nothing.

I promise to follow these instructions. Each day, for 14 days, I read this Verity at least two times, first thing in the morning and last thing at night. Each morning I read The Verity in silence then I sit still in silence for five minutes. In the evening I read it again but this time in a robust voice with great enthusiasm, charging it with emotion. And what do I think about? Things in my life that I am grateful for. I repeat this ritual twice a day for 14 days before moving to the next Verity. I spend 2 weeks with each Verity, influencing my subconscious, growing my character and Standing Tall so the Map becomes mine and so do the 13 Riches. My mind may drift often onto other things during these 5 minutes of sitting absolutely still and silent yet I observe this and come back to my blessings. Again. And again. My concentration improves daily.

And what of affluence today?

Kindness is an expression of gratitude. Right *now* I begin to identify kindness in everyone, everywhere and everything. I bring kindness with me mentally and physically. My manners are a wonderful, beautiful expression of kindness. In every encounter I give something; love, a compliment, a blessing, a hug… it does not matter if what I give is physical or thoughts. What matters is my awareness of the chance to give *now* and the sincerity of my giving.

I always remember that I am giving without expectation of reciprocity. I attempt to commit at least 2 random acts of kindness every day without getting caught. I begin to see, day by day, more kindness in the world and my gratitude grows. At the end of every day I jot down 3 things I am grateful for, past or present, before my nightly reading of the verity and my silently sitting still. My daily 3 gratitudes are always different. This keeps me alert and connects me to abundance *now*. Like many before me it will seem like I am merely writing a list yet soon I begin to notice I am feeling gratitude. I have a grateful heart.

And what of Standing Tall?

The secret of The Map is that it is 3-dimensional! I must Stand Tall to see beyond the distractions and temptations that block the 13 riches of life and see over the world's mirages of riches that attract those without character. Standing Tall is about growing the dormant greatness within myself, the greatness of my character. I am not Standing Tall to tower over others, but to be a beacon of gratitude, kindness and character. Character growth begins with my giving to myself and I do. I give myself a promise to read each Verity twice a day for two weeks and sit and think as directed. I sign the line below and speak the promise aloud at both readings, including my name. I begin *now* because *now* is the only place anything can happen and my future wealth is determined by what I do *now*.

_____

I am a grateful giver and I always keep my promises.

I give myself the gift of charting my progress, checking off each kept promise

Day 1 Promise

- ☐ AM read + 5 minute silent sit on gratitude
- ☐ PM read aloud + 5 minute silent sit on gratitude

Day 2 Promise

- ☐ AM read + 5 minute silent sit on gratitude
- ☐ PM read aloud + 5 minute silent sit on gratitude

Day 3 Promise

- ☐ AM read + 5 minute silent sit on gratitude
- ☐ PM read aloud + 5 minute silent sit on gratitude

Day 4 Promise

- ☐ AM read + 5 minute silent sit on gratitude
- ☐ PM read aloud + 5 minute silent sit on gratitude

Day 5 Promise

- ☐ AM read + 5 minute silent sit on gratitude
- ☐ PM read aloud + 5 minute silent sit on gratitude

Day 6 Promise

- ☐ AM read + 5 minute silent sit on gratitude
- ☐ PM read aloud + 5 minute silent sit on gratitude

Day 7 Promise

- ☐ AM read + 5 minute silent sit on gratitude
- ☐ PM read aloud + 5 minute silent sit on gratitude

Day 8 Promise

- ☐ AM read + 5 minute silent sit on gratitude
- ☐ PM read aloud + 5 minute silent sit on gratitude

Day 9 Promise

- ☐ AM read + 5 minute silent sit on gratitude
- ☐ PM read aloud + 5 minute silent sit on gratitude

Day 10 Promise

- ☐ AM read + 5 minute silent sit on gratitude
- ☐ PM read aloud + 5 minute silent sit on gratitude

Day 11 Promise

- ☐ AM read + 5 minute silent sit on gratitude
- ☐ PM read aloud + 5 minute silent sit on gratitude

Day 12 Promise

- ☐ AM read + 5 minute silent sit on gratitude
- ☐ PM read aloud + 5 minute silent sit on gratitude

Day 13 Promise

- ☐ AM read + 5 minute silent sit on gratitude
- ☐ PM read aloud + 5 minute silent sit on gratitude

Day 14 Promise

- ☐ AM read + 5 minute silent sit on gratitude
- ☐ PM read aloud + 5 minute silent sit on gratitude

The Second Verity

"The I"

Imagination

*I*feel grateful, my world is a little kinder each and every day. As gratitude moves into my heart and I give without expectation of reciprocity and become a better observer, more things to be grateful for are revealing themselves.

Gratitude is a cause, not an effect.

I am Standing Taller and developing humility. It's become clear to me that growing my character is the only passage to my greatness. This greatness is not to glorify me nor get notice from the world around me. Being great simply means I do my best with all tasks, all people, with the Verities and with myself. The reward is peace of mind. This peace of mind opens the window to my imagination. Living in my imagination leads to living a life of purpose, with purpose and on purpose.

I am a grateful giver and humble receiver.

Today I humbly receive the deeper wisdom about imagination and gratefully give myself the gift of regenerating my magnificent imagination.

I captured a tremendous insight from the First Verity about my life. I have created the life I chose with the decisions I have made, day to day, minute to minute. I Stand Tall here and celebrate this regardless of how I feel about the current circumstances, grateful to know I am creative. If I desire different circumstances I must make different decisions. I know the subconscious makes all the decisions and while I am influencing subconscious with enthusiastic repetitions, my future will be determined by my imagination not resolutions nor reconfiguring current circumstances.

The life I have in the future will be determined by the thoughts that I hold. The thoughts I hold are my intention. There are only two types of people in the world. Those who hold thoughts of their current circumstances and those who hold thoughts of the purposeful life they earnestly desire. Since thought charged with feeling creates my beliefs and my beliefs are the seat of my habits and my habits are what determines my actions and my actions create my circumstances I have a very simple decision to make.

Will I continue to focus on my circumstances which reinforce my current beliefs, actions, habits and the life I have or will I create a new intention in my imagination, charge that purposeful intention with feeling and render unto myself new beliefs, habits and actions?

More specifically, will I fight to keep the life I have, determined to live by the mundane precedents my current mind firmly holds or surrender to my heart's desire, open up to adventure and live by the progress new ideas and thoughts dictate?

What will I decide? The great wisdom within the Second Verity makes this decision easy to make and easy to live by.

Life is without meaning, it always has been and it always will be.

While others foolishly waste their imagination on trying to understand the meaning of life I *now* know that life… simply is. That is it. There is no mystery, no riddle to solve and no deep philosophical meaning. Life does not give me meaning because life has no meaning. The only meaning my life will ever have is the meaning I give to it. I give meaning to my life by deciding what my purpose is and that purpose is found in my imagination.

I choose progress over precedent, adventure over comfortable routine. I listen to the whisperings of my heart. I have made my decision! This simple decision opens up an infinite field of possibilities in my imagination and avoids the inescapable trap of trying to fix what is in the past. I no longer measure life by the number of breaths I take but by the moments that take my breath away!

And where is this pathway to moments of wonder, excitement and purpose? My imagination. I master my imagination by using it as the light to discover and penetrate new worlds. Everything that mankind has ever accomplished or achieved was first a thought, an idea that germinated in one's imagination. Repetition of that thought, charged with feeling, created a clear mental picture followed by manifestation. This is true of the clothes I am now wearing, chair I am sitting in, home I live in and the village the home sits in. It is true of all that exists and *it is my imagination that will birth the ideal that becomes my future.* Every artist, discoverer, inventor and author used this breathtaking instrument of the mind to create marvels and miracles.

The Master Architect created a masterpiece in me and I now make of my life the same. I am the artist of the picture my life becomes. Its beauty is drawn from my imagination. I am the inventor; inventing the life I desire and using my imagination to get a clear mental picture of that ideal. I am the discoverer of new worlds for the person my heart has been yearning me to be. I am the author of my future and no longer surrender the pen to others when writing my future.

It is my imagination that will birth the ideal that becomes my future. And how am I to do this today? By exercising my imagination, I cultivate my ideal. I begin with the question only my heart can answer and then let my imagination go to work creating a clearer and clearer picture of my ideal self and my world. The question is this; "what am I pretending not to know?" While my parents, schooling, institutions and my culture all have ideas for what is best for me I know, in my heart, my ideal. I no longer pretend I do not know my heart's desire.

As I live with this verity for 14 days, reading it twice daily and then sitting in silence, I do new things with my imagination to exercise it. First, I sit for 6 minutes after both the silent read in the morning and the hardy, out loud reading at night. I begin each sit with the following statement, *"I know my ideal. It manifests because it is good for me, takes no one else's good, is founded in service to others and represents the Source of All Good with respect."* I then direct my imagination to get a clear mental picture of that ideal. Since my subconscious does not know the difference between something vividly imagined and something that actually happens I direct my imagination in the following way. I imagine entering a familiar café in the marketplace where my best friend is sitting at a table. We greet each other as we always do and begin our conversation, as we normally do. When my friend asked *"what's new?"* I share this great adventure I've just completed, describing in detail my ideal as if it has already happened. I see the joy on my friend's face, the happiness in my friend's eyes, and I hear our shouts of glee and laughter. Each time I sit my concentration improves and I see more and more detail. Same café, we are both wearing the same garments but my imagination notices more detail in the café and in each other. I see, feel, smell, touch and hear the experience during each sit in more and more detail. *It is my imagination that will birth the ideal that becomes my future.* I use my imagination to create my life's intention. On the last day with this Verity I take a small card and write out my now vividly clear intention and include the feelings I know I experience upon its attainment.

I use my imagination to vitalize my intention daily and I always keep my promises.

I chart my progress, Standing Tall in promises

Day 1 Verity "I" Promise
- ☐ AM read + 6 min. silent sit with imagination
- ☐ PM read aloud + 6 minute silent sit with imagination

Day 2 Verity "I" Promise
- ☐ AM read + 6 min. silent sit with imagination
- ☐ PM read aloud + 6 minute silent sit with imagination

Day 3 Verity "I" Promise
- ☐ AM read + 6 min. silent sit with imagination
- ☐ PM read aloud + 6 minute silent sit with imagination

Day 4 Verity "I" Promise
- ☐ AM read + 6 min. silent sit with imagination
- ☐ PM read aloud + 6 minute silent sit with imagination

Day 5 Verity "I" Promise
- ☐ AM read + 6 min. silent sit with imagination
- ☐ PM read aloud + 6 minute silent sit with imagination

Day 6 Verity "I" Promise
- ☐ AM read + 6 min. silent sit with imagination
- ☐ PM read aloud + 6 minute silent sit with imagination

Day 7 Verity "I" Promise
- ☐ AM read + 6 min. silent sit with imagination
- ☐ PM read aloud + 6 minute silent sit with imagination

Day 8 Verity "I" Promise
- ☐ AM read + 6 min. silent sit with imagination
- ☐ PM read aloud + 6 minute silent sit with imagination

Day 9 Verity "I" Promise
- ☐ AM read + 6 min. silent sit with imagination
- ☐ PM read aloud + 6 minute silent sit with imagination

Day 10 Verity "I" Promise
- ☐ AM read + 6 min. silent sit with imagination
- ☐ PM read aloud + 6 minute silent sit with imagination

Day 11 Verity "I" Promise
- ☐ AM read + 6 min. silent sit with imagination
- ☐ PM read aloud + 6 minute silent sit with imagination

Day 12 Verity "I" Promise
- ☐ AM read + 6 min. silent sit with imagination
- ☐ PM read aloud + 6 minute silent sit with imagination

Day 13 Verity "I" Promise
- ☐ AM read + 6 min. silent sit with imagination
- ☐ PM read aloud + 6 minute silent sit with imagination

Day 14 Verity "I" Promise
- ☐ AM read + 6 min. silent sit with imagination
- ☐ PM read aloud + 6 minute silent sit with imagination

KEY: I write out my intention on a card 3x5 or smaller card 3 times. I write it in the present tense and include the feelings I experience when it is attained. I always carry one, place one by my bed and one by my workplace.

The Third Verity

"The X"

Release Limiting Beliefs

I am grateful, my world is a little kinder each and every day. My grateful heart takes joy in giving without expectation of reciprocity. Becoming a better observer I see more things to be grateful for revealing themselves. The resources, ideas, people, opportunities and encouragement needed to manifest my intention are only a fraction of the growing prosperity the Source of All Good is providing daily. Gratitude is a cause, not an effect and I am in the flow. I am a grateful giver and humble receiver.

While my imagination births my intention and concentration coupled repetitiously reading my card several times daily vigorously are paramount to influencing my subconscious mind, it is my attention, minute-to-minute, that manifests my intention. I must detach from the outcome and avoid the destroyer of many wonderful intentions for multitudes of people over the centuries. And what is that destroyer? Limiting beliefs. Limiting beliefs are all that stand between the 13 riches, my intention and myself. I continue to grow thus being able to see over all limiting beliefs. *I am ready to release what I no longer need so I can receive what I desire.*

In several villages they use pots with a small hole in the side to capture monkeys simply by placing bananas in the vessel then sealing the top. The monkey can easily slip his hand in and grab hold of a banana but when holding the banana, he cannot get his hand out. All the monkey must do to free himself is let go of the banana. Sadly, he never does and capturing monkeys is easy for the villagers. To receive the bounty within the Verities, grow in tall character, garner the 13 riches and my intention, I must understand that all limiting beliefs must be released. The monkey gives up his freedom for a banana and this teaches me a great lesson. He cannot have the banana and his freedom. *I am ready to release what I no longer need so I can receive what I desire.*

Some of these limiting beliefs are easy to see, some I have denied while others hide in my blind spots. Should I look for these limiting beliefs? Of course not! The Great Law of Growth teaches me that which I identify will multiply. Looking for limiting beliefs in my thoughts grows them by giving them power. Holding onto limiting beliefs impedes my purpose and would mimic the monkey holding a banana. I am not a monkey who is unable to process the difference between a meal and freedom. *It is my imagination that will birth the ideal that becomes my future* and I now understand that limiting beliefs hobble this great gift.

And then how do I release all limiting beliefs? I begin by acknowledging that the mechanism between my ears is unrivaled, it is magnificent and it works perfectly. Those that raised me, and the institutions that trained me, did their best to protect me yet I never learned the great Laws of the faultless mind I have been given by the Creator. This has rendered me unaware of the immense power within the domain of my mind and left me inexperienced in harnessing its power. Negative thought patterns and poor mental habits I've unknowingly copied from others have bred limiting beliefs. *I am ready to release what I no longer need so I can receive what I desire.*

How do I release all my known and unknown limiting beliefs? By learning and applying the Law of Substitution, another Great Law of the Mind. This Law is simple; the mind can hold only one thought at a time. By freeing my mind from attachment and ego, my improving concentration accelerates to focused attention and that hastens the manifesting of my intention. I begin by judging no one.

All judgment I have is a form of attachment to the person I am and prevents me from becoming the one I was always intended to be, the one who Stands Tall and acquires wealth unilaterally. This judgment shows itself dozens of time daily in the form of opinion. Each opinion I am tempted to give verbally I do not. Instead, I give love and respect. As I observe how many opinions I have, and I slip often the first day or two, I laugh and celebrate my discovery. I know that giving no opinions is releasing limiting beliefs. Stopping verbally is fairly easy for me, the real struggle will be the opinions in my mind. I know that eventually I emerge victorious with this new thought habit that is replacing limiting beliefs. *I am ready to release what I no longer need so I can receive what I desire.*

There is no greater limiting belief than negative thought. I embrace this next step known as the *mental diet*. I monitor my thoughts with a steely determination to no longer hold negative thoughts. It is here that the Law of Substitution pays immense dividends. Whenever I cuss, express impatience, anger at another outwardly or have a negative thought at all, I reach for my highest intention. I may use the card I wrote or my developing imagination. *I have a choice now.* I can hold that negative thought and let it fortify my limiting beliefs or I can substitute a different thought; my heart's desire… or the Creator or a wonderful moment in my life. I may slip often the first few days but I now possess a truth of colossal power; by stringing together 7 or more days without a negative thought, word or an opinion, all limiting beliefs I may have will eventually atrophy. It feels so wonderful that I now begin a life without negative thought, improving daily. Why? *I am ready to release what I no longer need so I can receive what I desire.*

As always I read the Verity two times daily and always read it at night out loud with intense feeling. This two weeks, however, I live an enlightening metaphor. Instead of sitting quietly after my morning read, I take several pebbles and place them in my left shoe. I walk for 4 minutes and think of all the things in my life that are unsatisfactory, what is wrong with my home, friends, government... all the wrongs. I walk for 4 minutes, limping along and feeling the discomfort as my mind judges others. I stop, empty my shoe of the pebbles and walk for another 4 minutes. This time I think about things that go right, my intention, good things that have happened to me, things I am grateful for. At the completion of this walk I reflect for 30 seconds on my moving metaphor. Which was more pleasurable? Do I understand those pebbles are nothing compared to the power of negative thought? Do I now see how easily, by letting go of the pebbles and switching my mind to positive that I have this power of choice at my disposal? After the evening read I sit still for 6 minutes and in the first minute I relive that morning walk, both ways. I spend the last 5 minutes of the silent sit celebrating my improvement, thinking about my intention and bewildered by the power I have discovered within myself to control my thoughts.

I hold only positive thoughts and always keep my promises.

I'm Standing Taller, keeping my promises

Day 1 Verity "R" Promise
- ☐ AM read + 8 minute walk with pebbles
- ☐ PM read aloud + 6 minute silent sit

Day 2 Verity "R" Promise
- ☐ AM read + 8 minute walk with pebbles
- ☐ PM read aloud + 6 minute silent sit

Day 3 Verity "R" Promise
- ☐ AM read + 8 minute walk with pebbles
- ☐ PM read aloud + 6 minute silent sit

Day 4 Verity "R" Promise
- ☐ AM read + 8 minute walk with pebbles
- ☐ PM read aloud + 6 minute silent sit

Day 5 Verity "R" Promise
- ☐ AM read + 8 minute walk with pebbles
- ☐ PM read aloud + 6 minute silent sit

Day 6 Verity "R" Promise
- ☐ AM read + 8 minute walk with pebbles
- ☐ PM read aloud + 6 minute silent sit

Day 7 Verity "R" Promise
- ☐ AM read + 8 minute walk with pebbles
- ☐ PM read aloud + 6 minute silent sit

Day 8 Verity "R" Promise
- ☐ AM read + 8 minute walk with pebbles
- ☐ PM read aloud + 6 minute silent sit

Day 9 Verity "R" Promise
- ☐ AM read + 8 minute walk with pebbles
- ☐ PM read aloud + 6 minute silent sit

Day 10 Verity "R" Promise
- ☐ AM read + 8 minute walk with pebbles
- ☐ PM read aloud + 6 minute silent sit

Day 11 Verity "R" Promise
- ☐ AM read + 8 minute walk with pebbles
- ☐ PM read aloud + 6 minute silent sit

Day 12 Verity "R" Promise
- ☐ AM read + 8 minute walk with pebbles
- ☐ PM read aloud + 6 minute silent sit

Day 13 Verity "R" Promise
- ☐ AM read + 8 minute walk with pebbles
- ☐ PM read aloud + 6 minute silent sit

Day 14 Verity "R" Promise
- ☐ AM read + 8 minute walk with pebbles
- ☐ PM read aloud + 6 minute silent si

The Fourth Verity

"The A"

Action Focused and Attachment Free

I am grateful and feeling more and more passion daily for my intention. I have heard the whisperings of my heart's desire and each day my actions demonstrate loyalty to my intention. Life is returning to me a marvelous feeling of sincere purpose. How has this happened so quickly? The Law of Environment is the secret that those who have held the Verities know. And what is this Law of Environment?

That which belongs in an environment will show up and grow just as that which does not belong in an environment will atrophy.

My first action daily is to protect this new and splendidly constructive environment within my mind by soaking it with a verbal barrage of gratitude. Making this my first action of each day causes even more things to be grateful for and that includes all that will be needed to manifest my intention and continue the gladdening feeling of a life lived with purpose.

Penguins and polar bears thrive in the bitter cold yet do not show up in the desert lest they would perish. This is true in all of nature. Since I too am part of nature, it is therefore also true of the one thing I have control over, the environment of my mind. With great care I cradle this limitless environment within myself. I cultivate a majestic setting that continually invites positive thoughts, helpful ideas, kindness, gratitude, kindred souls and love. Since this is my authentic nature those attributes truly belong and by the Law of Environment they must show up and quickly flourish because I am diligent in protecting my mind's environment. Fear, doubt, insecurity and limiting beliefs try to slip into my constructive mental environment from time to time but quickly wither and die like roses would in the Arctic.

While having a feeling of purpose is uplifting and pleases me, the wisdom of this Verity teaches me that I must take action without hesitation on the ideas that move my intention to reality and I do. My daily deeds are a statement of who I am. Standing Tall, I walk my talk so my thoughts of purpose and my actions are identical. My actions shout loudly to my purpose and are a clear indication to all, and to myself, I thoughtfully live my life both *with purpose and on purpose.*

How do I know what actions to take to improve myself, my relationships and grow my purpose into a vital reality? There lies within me greatness. To grow that greatness I must do my best. To do my best, I must know what to do. To know specifically what to do in all situations, I question myself constantly from the perspective of the person I have imagined myself to be when thinking of my intention. This is the one question that instantly sorts all ideas, eliminates confusion about what to do and eventually converts the Verities and The Map to the 13 Riches from mere words into my rightful territory.

"What would the person I intend to become do next?"

The forefather of all things, of all achievement is thought... and then matching action. Since things like fear, doubt and procrastination wither in the environment of positive expectation I have established within, I find myself acting instantly once I ask myself *"what would the person I intend to become do next?"* While some actions will be different or be uncomfortable at first, I now possess a great truth of this Verity; the risk of action is dwarfed by the risk of comfortable inaction.

Since I have been faithful with the Verities I am protected from acting out on each and every positive idea I hear. The world is full of temptations and distractions. It is full of wonder, of great things, of useless short cuts, of mirages promising happiness, of good ideas and fine businesses. How can I tell the difference and withstand all distractions? Humility!

I have made my choice, stated my intention, declared my purpose and know it is of great service to others, honoring the *Source of All Good.* My focus is likened to a magnifying glass that will only create combustion when held still. I hold my focus on what will advance only three things; my relationship to the *Source of All Good,* to my loved ones and to my service driven purpose. And are they not one in the same? Should good things cross my path I have the humility required to know if it is not advancing my purpose that it simply is not mine. *"What would the person I intend to become do next?"*

And the greatest of all sagacity within this Verity resides in being detached rather than attached. Attachment to yesterday mandates I remain mired in precedent, prevents growth and I remain unchanged. Attachment to the outcome of tomorrow stymies discovery of the rich resources and lessons needed that are found only in the *now.* Like a moving magnifying glass, attachment to either scuttles my attention and my attention is what determines my intention. With a steady magnifying-glass-focus and detachment, my actions are great because I pay attention to the *now*. *Now*. *Now* is all there is. *Now* is all there ever was and *now* is all there ever will be.

Each action generated by asking myself *"what would the person I intend to become do next?"* moves my intention closer in one of two ways. It either advances my purpose or teaches me something profound that serves to fulfill my purpose later. I am attachment free, reveling in continuous moments of uncertainty; I fully understand there is no new wisdom found in what I am attached to and already know. Standing Tall in the dynamic field of uncertainty finds the new insights and infinite potential needed to actualize my purpose easily.

And how do I uncover these lessons and resources as expressed with grace from the *Source of All Good* so I may convert them into service and make my dreams come true? With action! My smile opens the door to the grace of people. My manners sparkle so earnestly they invite me into their lives and share their gifts. As with all creatures, like attracts like and being a grateful giver triggers a tidal wave of all I need that day if I pay attention.

I promise to sign and read this Verity twice daily. Living with this verity for 14 days sees the time between a purpose advancing idea and positive detached action vanish. I hug my mate *now* when the idea crosses my mind, not later. I help a friend *now* when the idea hits, not later. When I am doing business I always know what the person I intend to become should be doing to drive the business. I do it first, I do it better and I do it more often each day. I reward my behavior and remain detached from the results. For just as the sun rises in the east, so do great results show up if I engage only in the behaviors of the person I intend to become.

Before my morning read I repeat the phrase "do it now" 25 times aloud with all the feeling I can muster. I then sit still for 6 minutes and in my mind I see myself taking action on the primary behaviors that advance my intention. My mind may drift but I notice my concentration is getting better and better. If it drifts I smile and come right back to imagining the actions I take, seeing myself in motion and picturing positive performance of my actions. I conclude the morning sit by repeating "do it now" 25 times again with greater feeling!

After the aloud evening read, I sit for another 6 minutes. During this sit I review my day, thinking only about two things. First, I ask myself in my mind, "what did I do right?" In my mind I list everything I did right no matter how small it may seem. I then ask myself, "what could I improve?" This unearths priceless insights. These actions coupled with my habit of keeping all promises have my character Standing Taller each day.

I repeat "do it now" 25 times, twice a day and I always keep my promises.

What would the person I intend to become do next? Chart my promise keeping and repeat "do it now" 25x at least twice per day

Day 1 Verity "A" Promise
- □ AM read + 6 minute sit, picturing action
- □ PM read aloud + 6 minute sit, 2 questions

Day 2 Verity "A" Promise
- □ AM read + 6 minute sit, picturing action
- □ PM read aloud + 6 minute sit, 2 questions

Day 3 Verity "A" Promise
- □ AM read + 6 minute sit, picturing action
- □ PM read aloud + 6 minute sit, 2 questions

Day 4 Verity "A" Promise
- □ AM read + 6 minute sit, picturing action
- □ PM read aloud + 6 minute sit, 2 questions

Day 5 Verity "A" Promise
- □ AM read + 6 minute sit, picturing action
- □ PM read aloud + 6 minute sit, 2 questions

Day 6 Verity "A" Promise
- □ AM read + 6 minute sit, picturing action
- □ PM read aloud + 6 minute sit, 2 questions

Day 7 Verity "A" Promise
- □ AM read + 6 minute sit, picturing action
- □ PM read aloud + 6 minute sit, 2 questions

Day 8 Verity "A" Promise
- □ AM read + 6 minute sit, picturing action
- □ PM read aloud + 6 minute sit, 2 questions

Day 9 Verity "A" Promise
- □ AM read + 6 minute sit, picturing action
- □ PM read aloud + 6 minute sit, 2 questions

Day 10 Verity "A" Promise
- □ AM read + 6 minute sit, picturing action
- □ PM read aloud + 6 minute sit, 2 questions

Day 11 Verity "A" Promise
- □ AM read + 6 minute sit, picturing action
- □ PM read aloud + 6 minute sit, 2 questions

Day 12 Verity "A" Promise
- □ AM read + 6 minute sit, picturing action
- □ PM read aloud + 6 minute sit, 2 questions

Day 13 Verity "A" Promise
- □ AM read + 6 minute sit, picturing action
- □ PM read aloud + 6 minute sit, 2 questions

Day 14 Verity "A" Promise
- □ AM read + 6 minute sit, picturing action
- □ PM read aloud + 6 minute sit, 2 questions

The Fifth Verity

"The First F"

First Things First

I am growing in character and each day I feel myself Standing Taller, pushing my realized and growing potential to new heights with action. Daily I am reaching far beyond limits others and I myself have set. I am certain the 13 Riches of Life on The Map become a radiant confirmation of the immense power within I am beginning to harness. While I am a person of action I fully comprehend there is a significant difference between activity and productivity. How do I ensure that each and every action I take is in line with the person I am intended to become? How do I move forward with confidence *before* I arise in the morning so that my actions are congruent with the real treasures my limitless potential promises?

I keep first things first.

A double-minded person is unstable in many ways. What is a double-minded person? One who changes their philosophy and priorities depending on circumstances rather than keeping first things first. Why does this make one unstable?

If we don't stand for something, we will fall for anything.

I am grateful for this Verity's wisdom and my indelible decision to keep first things first. How do I permanently establish my priorities? How do I remain open to everything and dance with confidence in the wisdoms of uncertainty? *I keep first things first.*

There once was a man who did not complete his work during the hours allotted so he brought it home. Working at his desk early Saturday morning his young son bounded into the room where the man was toiling. The boy wanted the father to play with him as usual. The father explained he had to work. The boy's lip began to quiver as he tried to hold back his tears. The father, desperate to ease the boy's pain got an idea to delay the playtime. He grabbed a drawing of a world map, held it up and summoned the boy to his lap. The father said, "I will make a puzzle out of this and as soon as you put it together I will play with you." The father tore the map into many pieces. He believed it would take quite some time as the boy had no knowledge of the world's geography. The father was relieved as the boy left the room with dozens of scraps of paper. In less than 2 minutes the boy was back and the map was put together perfectly. "Can we play now like you promised Father?" The father was stunned as he rose from his desk to keep his word yet could not help but ask the boy how he put that map together so quickly. "Oh, it was easy father. When you first held the map up I noticed the other side had the drawing of a man's face. I knew if I got the man put together right, the world would be right."

I keep first things first.

If I am right within my heart, my world without will be right also. And how do I make my world within right? My spiritual fitness is always the first priority. All my actions from this day forward are based on honoring *The Source of All Good.* I have begun this process by sitting still daily and in silence. I expand this habit to include communicating daily with *The Source.* Prayer is talking to *The Source of All Good* as I understand it and meditation is listening to *The Source.* I earnestly vow to keep my world within spiritually fit. *I keep first things first.* I raise my conscious contact with *The Source* daily by asking for only three things. First, I ask for greater powers of observation so I may become more aware of chances to serve others. Secondly, I ask to be reminded to give a gift to each and every encounter as directed in the *First Verity.* Lastly I ask for the strength of character that I may respect the rights of others before my own feelings and the feelings of others before my rights. Then, I listen with an open heart.

Each Friday I gather my loved ones and thank them for their support during the week. I remind them and myself that while my work and purpose are vitally important that nothing is more important to me than each of them. I then proceed to schedule time with each of my loved ones. It could be a walk with my spouse, a game with my son and imaginary tea party with my daughter. What is most important about each activity? I am fully present, abstaining from all else except the activity. I conclude this meeting by scheduling a time for all of us to love and enjoy one another together. I then retreat to plan my work for the upcoming week.

And what of work? Every business or occupation has one or two critical behaviors that drive success. From asking myself "what would the person I intend to become do next?" and my experience, I already know what must be scheduled first. I make the time to improve by gathering knowledge and honing my skills. And where and when do I accomplish this? The same place all champions are found, the extra mile. I have the energy to go the extra mile because I master this Verity, keeping first things first. I now realize that giving things up is actually moving up! As my connection to *The Source* grows, my need for childish distractions that serve no purpose for *The Source*, my loved ones, myself or my work fades away.

While others shift their priorities often and flounder daily, the habit of *keeping first things first* becomes ingrained and unshakeable within the environment of my mind. Each day, each sit in silence is preceded by a few minutes of listening to *The Source*. I am fully cognizant these few seconds spent asking to be a better observer, a gift giver of love to all and respectful to the rights and feelings of others before my own, followed by two minutes of listening with my heart open, is a minuscule price to pay for the 13 Riches of Life. *Keeping first things first* grows me for my priorities are aligned with Universal Mind. Once I complete these 2 minutes I think of the largest structure in my village and spend 4 minutes contemplating it. In my mind I see the space before the structure existed. I go back further to the workers who built it, the laborers who brought the material to the workers... back to those who mined the materials... and back to the architect who designed it... and the debates about whether or not it should be built... and further back still to the mind that originally declared the intention. This process, repeated twice daily in my silent sit, gets more and more detailed in my mind. Herein lies the deeper wisdom of this *Verity*. This changes me by yielding cosmic insight to all that is in my world. I no longer see end results but rather intention manifested step-by- step by those who, like myself, *keep first things first.*

I promise to keep first things first and I always keep my promises

75

I spend 2 minutes with The Source prior to exercising my mind with the Fifth Verity

Day 1 Verity "First F" Promise
  ☐ AM read + 4 minutes on largest structure
  ☐ PM read aloud + 4 on largest structure

Day 2 Verity "First F " Promise
  ☐ AM read + 4 minutes on largest structure
  ☐ PM read aloud + 4 on largest structure

Day 3 Verity "First F " Promise
  ☐ AM read + 4 minutes on largest structure
  ☐ PM read aloud + 4 on largest structure

Day 4 Verity "First F " Promise
  ☐ AM read + 4 minutes on largest structure
  ☐ PM read aloud + 4 on largest structure

Day 5 Verity "First F " Promise
  ☐ AM read + 4 minutes on largest structure
  ☐ PM read aloud + 4 on largest structure

Day 6 Verity "First F " Promise
  ☐ AM read + 4 minutes on largest structure
  ☐ PM read aloud + 4 on largest structure

Day 7 Verity "First F " Promise
  ☐ AM read + 4 minutes on largest structure
  ☐ PM read aloud + 4 on largest structure

Day 8 Verity "First F " Promise
  ☐ AM read + 4 minutes on largest structure
  ☐ PM read aloud + 4 on largest structure

Day 9 Verity "First F " Promise
  ☐ AM read + 4 minutes on largest structure
  ☐ PM read aloud + 4 on largest structure

Day 10 Verity "First F " Promise
  ☐ AM read + 4 minutes on largest structure
  ☐ PM read aloud + 4 on largest structure

Day 11 Verity "First F " Promise
  ☐ AM read + 4 minutes on largest structure
  ☐ PM read aloud + 4 on largest structure

Day 12 Verity "First F " Promise
  ☐ AM read + 4 minutes on largest structure
  ☐ PM read aloud + 4 on largest structure

Day 13 Verity "First F " Promise
  ☐ AM read + 4 minutes on largest structure
  ☐ PM read aloud + 4 on largest structure

Day 14 Verity "First F " Promise
  ☐ AM read + 4 minutes on largest structure
  ☐ PM read aloud + 4 on largest structure

The Sixth Verity

"The Second F"

Made First Class by First Class

I was made first class by first class and I can go first class if I render first class service without expectation of reciprocity. Each day I move closer to consistently displaying my infinite potential with sincere humility. Within me is the Primal Power of Being; it is a reservoir of inexhaustible positive energy, divine ideas, greatness and unimaginable power. There is nothing to do to acquire the Primal Power. I was born with it. To use the power all that is required is to begin to consider how to use it. I now claim my birthright and align myself with this Power. I draw it out of myself utilizing the Ancient Verities and harness it for the greatest good. I shall always Stand Tall in this truth of the Primal Power of Being and become great now.

How do I begin to consider harnessing the power that yields greatness?

Shipwrecked sailors, in an open raft, were drifting in the Atlantic Ocean. They had no water and were suffering the traumas of thirst. After 3 days another boat came upon them and they desperately clamored for water. The newcomers yelled back, "Throw down your bucket!" How sadistic this must have sounded. The thirsty mariners keep asking for water only to hear the same response over and over, "Throw down your bucket!" Finally, out of desperation, one of the parched sailors tossed down a bucket and pulled up fresh, clean, glistening water. Despite being out of sight of land, they had been drifting in the estuary system of the Amazon River, which pushes fresh water several miles out to sea.

My greatness and the power to put that greatness on display is within me. Like the sailors I need only exercise both the Art of Recognition and the Act of Recognition. I recognize greatness within and act on it. Greatness is doing the best of which I am capable with each thought and subsequent action.

And do I engage in the Art of Recognition?

I recognize that *The Source of All Good* has made the world perfect. The same is true of all people, including me. I can decide to see the world as perfect for its *current stage of evolvement* or I can see it as decaying. I cannot see it both ways. The same is true of all people, including me; **perfect yet incomplete.** Like others who "throw down their bucket" I am excited about helping evolve and complete the perfecting of the world's evolvement by doing my best with the gifts and resources within myself.

This is the great discovery that inspires me to break from the pack of the fearful followers and Stand Tall in the Primal Truth of Being and thus become a fearless victor. I fully comprehend the same two great truths all the holders of this most powerful Verity have unraveled over the millenniums.

First, all people are created equal and second, there are no common people. I now recognize *The Source of All Good* gave **all people** control over just one thing, not three things, not seven things, just one thing; *thought.* Our thoughts, held and acted upon determine who we are. Since this ability to control thought is given to all people, we are all equal and can all do great things. All that has been available to great people is available to all people. This, then, is the key in the Art of Recognition.

And how do I engage in the Act of Recognition?

By controlling my *thoughts*, I can express my individual greatness, experience wonder and manifest wealth in all areas of life. My will, from this day forward, is used exclusively to observe *my thoughts* and then direct them to the benefit of all. Thought, held and entertained, is the only true measure of a man or a woman. My thoughts, nurtured, become charged with feelings to form my beliefs. My actions, dictated by my beliefs, are a precise depiction of my thoughts. And just as the seasons know exactly when to change, if my thoughts are great then so too will be my actions. I need only act on the limitless reservoir of power within to think great things and do great things.

While others may grapple with the idea of personal greatness, I move forward daily with humility, not judgment. Being great means doing the best that I am capable of doing with what I have been given to work with. I do this knowing that being great is its own reward and done to experience peace of mind, not self-glorification. I will never rest until my good is better and my better is best. I am the light of the world *now*, letting *The Source* shine through me. When I do this I become transparent to the transcendent my presence makes all those who engage with me feel safe, secure and treasured. I was made first class by first class and render first class service to all so they may be inspired to think great things, do great things and be great too. I was made first class by first class.

I now know *The Source* is not merely loving, but is love itself. I represent that love with every thought and action. This love flowing through me serves as a constant encouragement to all of the infinite potential within each of us and that each of us can be great. There are just two steps to unleash the Primal Power within and Stand Tall in character. I do both now.

The First Step? I release all resentments with love. Resentments are the only barriers within the channel the Primal Power runs through. Snakebites do not kill people, the venom does. Real or imagined, old or new, I forgive everyone for everything and anything. I free myself with forgiveness and thus open the channel of infinite love. I feel the Primal Power rush in, ready to be harnessed.

The Second Step? It is found within the energy that runs all things, that loves all things. I am surrounded by this secret but was unaware until now.

What is this secret?

Harmony.

Grass is grass, always. Birds are birds, always. They are in perfect harmony with their true nature; they are what they were intended to be. To be great I need only be in harmony with my true nature, that which I have always been intended to be. I was made first class by first class and render first class service.

How can I be certain I am in harmony with my true nature?

If my intention is good for me, takes no one else's good and is of service to the greater good I am in harmony with *The Source*. This is true of me for I have heard my heart's desire, know it is in harmony and I have become harmonious with my own true nature by acting without hesitation to the heralding of my heart.

And where will I find the courage, energy and resources to meet these lofty desires? *I can do all things through The Source, which strengthens me.*

After each of my two daily reads of this Verity I contemplate harmony in nature, thinking of how all things behave true to what they were intended to be. I am flabbergasted by the obvious; grass does not try to grow, it just does. Birds fly, flowers bloom… and I am humbled more each day as I become aware the same is true of me, my character and the unbounded love I have to share.

I promise to sit silently, contemplating harmony and I always keep my promises

I spend 2 minutes with The Source prior to exercising my mind with the Sixth Verity
I always sit in silence for 6 minutes or more after reading the First Class Verity and contemplate harmony all around me.

Day 1 Verity "Second F" Promise
- ☐ AM read + 6 mins. contemplating harmony
- ☐ PM read aloud + 6mins. contemplating

Day 2 Verity "Second F" Promise
- ☐ AM read + 6 mins. contemplating harmony
- ☐ PM read aloud + 6mins. contemplating

Day 3 Verity "Second F" Promise
- ☐ AM read + 6 mins. contemplating harmony
- ☐ PM read aloud + 6mins. contemplating

Day 4 Verity "Second F" Promise
- ☐ AM read + 6 mins. contemplating harmony
- ☐ PM read aloud + 6mins. contemplating

Day 5 Verity "Second F" Promise
- ☐ AM read + 6 mins. contemplating harmony
- ☐ PM read aloud + 6mins. contemplating

Day 6 Verity "Second F" Promise
- ☐ AM read + 6 mins. contemplating harmony
- ☐ PM read aloud + 6mins. contemplating

Day 7 Verity "Second F" Promise
- ☐ AM read + 6 mins. contemplating harmony
- ☐ PM read aloud + 6mins. contemplating

Day 8 Verity "Second F" Promise
- ☐ AM read + 6 mins. contemplating harmony
- ☐ PM read aloud + 6mins. contemplating

Day 9 Verity "Second F" Promise
- ☐ AM read + 6 mins. contemplating harmony
- ☐ PM read aloud + 6mins. contemplating

Day 10 Verity "Second F" Promise
- ☐ AM read + 6 mins. contemplating harmony
- ☐ PM read aloud + 6mins. contemplating

Day 11 Verity "Second F" Promise
- ☐ AM read + 6 mins. contemplating harmony
- ☐ PM read aloud + 6mins. contemplating

Day 12 Verity "Second F" Promise
- ☐ AM read + 6 mins. contemplating harmony
- ☐ PM read aloud + 6mins. contemplating

Day 13 Verity "Second F" Promise
- ☐ AM read + 6 mins. contemplating harmony
- ☐ PM read aloud + 6mins. contemplating

Day 14 Verity "Second F" Promise
- ☐ AM read + 6 mins. contemplating harmony
- ☐ PM read aloud + 6mins. contemplatin

The Seventh Verity

"The E"

Enthusiasm

The last Verity, enthusiasm, is what gives vitality to my every action, to my intention and to my life each and every day. Enthusiasm is the charismatic zest that attracts all people, engages all people and infects all people positively. Enthusiasm is abundant within me. Is today the day my boundless enthusiasm is unleashed? Yes!

I am so excited because I know that the whole is far greater than the sum of the parts and mastering this final Verity helps me Stand Tall in character.

And how could I not be enthused? I began raising my consciousness with the hope of being able to understand and utilize The Map to the 13 Riches. Yet I have already acquired plentiful bounty I did not know already existed within me.

Gratitude, I now understand is a cause, not an effect. I love that my heart is grateful and more things to be grateful for pour into my life for me to give. As promised, the more I give the more I seem to receive. I am wealthier each day in meaningful ways.

Imagination is the only true bridge to enthusiasm. I have sharpened my imagination. No longer using my creative powers to try and rearrange the past, I now see clear mental pictures of my intention and the person I was always intended to be. I am thrilled with the discovery that I am creative. I am creating a life of purpose, living on purpose and with purpose.

Releasing all my limiting beliefs buoys my soul. Replacing judgment and opinion with love and respect has freed me from the bondage of ego. I cherish this gift and find myself bursting with joy at being able to control my thoughts.

Action is now taken towards my intention without hesitation. The person I intend to become knows what to do next and *I do it now* with confidence. The moments of hesitation the will advance my intention have vanished. No longer being attached to the past nor the outcome of the future amplifies my enthusiasm. I know that the infinite is found in the finite, in the moment. I am aware of wonder and there is nothing more exciting than being in the moment, fully experiencing my life.

ƒirst Things First keeps the world within me right and being right within makes the world without right. As my relationship with *The Source of All Good* and my family continues to improve as I do, a peace of mind envelops my being. This peace of mind is the fountainhead of my passion. This passion shows in every aspect of my spiritual life, family life and work life.

ƒirst class begins with thinking great things and I do. Because I think great things and hold those thoughts, my body follows and I do great things. I'm invigorated because all I have begun to develop was always within me. I can hardly contain my excitement when I consider what other treasures were given to me by my creator that I shall mine from the depths of my soul.

€nthusiasm in every fiber of my being now grows even stronger within as I unlock the deeper wisdoms of this last Verity. I begin with understanding the astuteness of utilizing a Giraffe to symbolize these Verities. I now see beyond the mere physicality of Standing Tall as a metaphor for growing my character tall and realize I am raising my consciousness to new heights. *My time has come.*

I stand on the precipice of an entirely different level of consciousness that galvanizes the Seven Ancient Verities. This raised consciousness fosters a compelling, ongoing, richly textured, sincere enthusiasm in me that sparks interest, evokes passion and inspires each person my life touches. I do this now for *my time has come.*

The Mesopotamians and Egyptians do not do eulogies when people die. They ask but one question to measure the quality of a life. Did he have passion? Did she have passion? I have great passion because I have been blessed to live with purpose and now live my life on purpose. I cannot wait for the sun to come up and confidently begin my day.

And how do I find this enthusiasm that propels me to leap from my bed with confidence? It is found with a deep and active understanding of an irrefutable truth.

Nothing, not even an army, can stop an idea whose time has come. My time has come.

What was once just a faint whispering in my heart has been transformed to an idea and nothing can stop an idea whose time has come. This idea is now my clear intention. Since my intention is in harmony with *The Source* and service driven for the greater good, nothing can stop it from manifesting. As such, my enthusiasm grows into electrifying passion.

Nothing, not even an army, can stop an idea whose time has come. My time has come.

I humbly accept that genius has been birthed within me. When an intention is in harmony with *The Source* and injected with love from a pure heart, genius is born. My heart is pure. I have placed love in my intention because its manifestation benefits those in my world and I know there is no logical end to the ripple effect of my good works. How could I be anything but enthusiastic knowing the Omnipotent, Omniscient Genius is Omnipresent within me? My enthusiasm is the activated spirit within. It surges through me, effortlessly transforming into energy and providing me the strength and willingness to take action without hesitation. This spirit within guides me to the perfect action and completing the perfect action fortifies my enthusiasm.

How do I know what is the perfect action when I am faced with infinite possibilities in conversations, in the work place and with my loved ones? This is the great secret of the enlightened. What is this great secret?

The Source that is omnipresent within me is omnipresent in all things.

By opening my heart to all things, even things that appear to be opposites, I transcend appearances and see *The Source* is omnipresent in everything. In the world's apparent kaleidoscope of differences there is a spot in my heart where I fully experience that everything is connected and I am connected to everything because the omnipresence of *The Source* is in all things and in me. It is here that everything becomes one and I become one with everything. In this domain where I cannot be divided, I open up to the perfect action with my heart, not with my head. When I release my mind and listen with my heart I become transparent to the transcendent and the *perfect action selects me,* draws me to it and I act perfectly in all situations without hesitation.

For the next 14 days I sit still and in silence for 7 minutes after each of my two daily readings of this Verity. I spend the first minute thinking of the affairs of the day, of my loved ones and how I can make their lives better today. For the next 6 minutes I listen with my heart and let the perfect action select me.

I promise to sit silently, listening with my heart. I always keep my promises

83

I spend 2 minutes with The Source prior to exercising my mind with the Seventh Verity.

I always sit in silence for 7 minutes or more after reading the Enthusiasm Verity.

I listen with my heart and let the perfect action select me.

Day 1 Verity "E" Promise
- □ AM read + sit, listen with my heart
- □ PM read aloud + listen with my heart

Day 2 Verity "E" Promise
- □ AM read + sit, listen with my heart
- □ PM read aloud + listen with my heart

Day 3 Verity "E" Promise
- □ AM read + sit, listen with my heart
- □ PM read aloud + listen with my heart

Day 4 Verity "E" Promise
- □ AM read + sit, listen with my heart
- □ PM read aloud + listen with my heart

Day 5 Verity "E" Promise
- □ AM read + sit, listen with my heart
- □ PM read aloud + listen with my heart

Day 6 Verity "E" Promise
- □ AM read + sit, listen with my heart
- □ PM read aloud + listen with my heart

Day 7 Verity "E" Promise
- □ AM read + sit, listen with my heart
- □ PM read aloud + listen with my heart

Day 8 Verity "E" Promise
- □ AM read + sit, listen with my heart
- □ PM read aloud + listen with my heart

Day 9 Verity "E" Promise
- □ AM read + sit, listen with my heart
- □ PM read aloud + listen with my heart

Day 10 Verity "E" Promise
- □ AM read + sit, listen with my heart
- □ PM read aloud + listen with my heart

Day 11 Verity "E" Promise
- □ AM read + sit, listen with my heart
- □ PM read aloud + listen with my heart

Day 12 Verity "E" Promise
- □ AM read + sit, listen with my heart
- □ PM read aloud + listen with my heart

Day 13 Verity ""E" Promise
- □ AM read + sit, listen with my heart
- □ PM read aloud + listen with my heart

Day 14 Verity "E" Promise
- □ AM read + sit, listen with my heart
- □ PM read aloud + listen with my heart

Chapter Fourteen

The Dinner, The Mirages, and The Map

So, let me just say that if you are here without spending two weeks with each Verity, that temptation is getting its way. I understand, really, I do. Temptation is really good at its job. I was tempted to rush ahead, to see what these 13 Riches were. The trouble is that, until we grow in character, we simply cannot see the 13 Riches. Well, I guess that isn't really accurate. What I mean is we cannot understand the value of most of the 13 Riches, until we find the real treasure... ourselves. So, I'm going to give you one more shot here and encourage you, as strongly as I can. If you did not follow the directions, please go back to the First Verity and spend fourteen days with each Verity, exactly as directed.

The Dinner

After Doc handed me the Verities on the lanai, I spent some time on Kauai before flying home. Fourteen weeks later, Doc flew to the Mainland. We met in San Francisco. Just like all the carriers of the Verities before me, I had the follow-up ritual with the one who passed them over to me. I was filled with gratitude as I sat in a Starbucks, waiting for Doc. Truth be told, I got there thirty minutes early, because I was bursting with excitement. I was hoping Doc would be early, too. He wasn't, but he did show up on time. We hugged; he grabbed a coffee and said, "Let's go," as he headed for the door.

"Where are we headed?" I asked. He pointed to a limo, and we climbed in. "Fancy, schmancy," I said.

"Hey, we're wealthy, right?" Doc responded. I stopped dead in my tracks. It was the first time in my life, my new life, that I became fully cognizant that I had found the priceless treasure. I had found me, the me I was always intended to be. He stopped, turned back to me, and then backtracked his steps towards me.

"Just got a little emotional hit, did ya?" he asked, placing his hand on my shoulder. I nodded, choked up.

Doc said, "Well, all you have to do to keep it...," and I interrupted and finished his sentence with, "is keep giving it away." Another heartfelt hug.

A long one.

We hopped into the limo, and Doc's answer to my question about where we were going was, "The tradition is that the passer of the Verities takes the new reader for a nice dinner and shares a couple of stories about some of the folks who these Verities may have passed through. Legend, fact, who knows. So, we're going to eat at a place special I picked out. I figured you had some questions about how Toni and Peter passed it to me."

As we crossed the Oakland Bay Bridge, I decided to just let it unfold. I told Doc I figured he'd tell me what he wanted to share and what I needed to know when he was ready. Of course, I figured he'd open right up. He did not. He seemed more interested in my opinion about baseball and the Red Sox pitching staff than talking about the Verities. I remember thinking how nice it would be if he were as chatty about the Verities as he was about baseball. So, we talked baseball, until I discovered we were pulling into the Oakland Zoo.

He got very quiet when the limo dropped us off at the front gate. Doc paid our way into the zoo and quickened his pace. He moved with confidence, not looking at the map they gave us. Doc wasn't looking at any signs posted, either. He knew where he was going, and, in another instant, I knew what we were going to see. The pace quickened even more as we headed up an incline.

"There he is! There's Joey," he was shouting, like a kid. Both his arms were pointing to a giraffe. He was almost running.

"Joey?" I asked.

"Yeah, Joey," he responded. "He's mine, sort of. I adopted him a few years back."

"Adopted?"

"Yeah, you know. A monthly pledge to support the zoo, and they let you pick one out," he explained, pulling a twenty-dollar bill from his wallet. "Why don't you grab us a couple hot dogs. Mustard only for me. Water, too. Please."

"And this is the big, nice, ceremonial dinner?" I figured he could take a little ribbing.

Turning towards me, Doc laughed and said, "What could possibly be nicer than this?"

I grabbed a couple dogs for each of us. We sat on a bench, facing Joey and all the other giraffes. We did not speak, just polished off our dinner. Doc was right. It couldn't be more perfect. Finally, he turned to me and told me about his fourteen-week dinner with Toni and Peter as best as he could remember from all those years ago...

"So I get to that Italian joint, the same place Toni, Peter and I had met fourteen weeks earlier. I was pretty pleased I'd kept the promises from Verity to Verity. They knew that I knew I was already feeling wealthy, connected to all things. I probably had a look similar to the one I saw on your face at Starbucks. Ya know?" He didn't wait for an answer.

Doc went on to tell me that Peter and Toni had exchanged a knowing smile when he had told them that he was feeling wealthy already. I knew what he meant. I found myself nodding as he shared that part of the conversation and their reaction. "So, then, I asked them if they had any thoughts they could share with me about The Map."

"And did they?" I asked.

"Sort of." Doc paused to think. "Yeah, I'd say they did, come to think of it. Funny thing, looking back on it, I sort of knew what they were going to tell me."

"Just work through them one at a time?" I asked.

"Sure, they told me that, but, then, Toni talked for a couple minutes about The Law of Growth," Doc said. "It was actually pretty funny, well, maybe not 'funny-funny' in the 'ha-ha' sense. Just odd, I guess, but it struck me as funny."

"And that was..." I prompted.

"Well, the best that I can recall, it went down like this: Toni told me about The Law of Growth, how the Riches on The Map are manifested by that great law of the mind. Then, she said something really important to me. She told me that I should not use the riches to try and overcome something. Like, don't think about losing weight to get healthy, just think about health. Not to heal, because, according to her, that is just dragging the problem with you. Then, she and Peter both started laughing."

"Why?" I asked.

"That's exactly what I asked," Doc said.

"And what did they say?" I was really curious by this point. Up until then, Doc had been talking to me while looking out at the giraffes. Now, he was looking right into my eyes, like he had when I first met him on Kauai. I'm sure it was the look, more than the words, that made me so curious... it was really the first time since we sat on that bench that he totally broke away from the giraffes.

"Well, it turns out that this guy, Rousseau, who lived in France in the 1700s, had the Verities. He had had them for quite a while—he was a great man, a big player in the Age of Enlightenment."

"I'm not familiar with that," I admitted.

"The Enlightenment was really the birth of human rights on a big scale. Rousseau said that to say the son of a slave is a slave is to deny that he is a man, which was not popular with the rich. He wrote a pretty amazing document, 'The Social Contract.' A big part of it was that no one should be so wealthy they can buy someone else, and no one so poor that they would sell themselves. It was a great document, elegantly crafted from the Verities and 13 Riches. This will sound familiar, he wrote 'liberty may be gained, but never recovered' ... really great stuff. You should check it out sometime. It's mind-blowing."

I must have had a quizzical look on my face because Doc busted out laughing. He said, "I'm not laughing at you, Mark. I think I had the exact same expression on my face, too. I remember wondering why they were talking about this guy from France in the 1700s, instead of The Map." He put his hand gently on my face and smiled.

"Anyway," Doc continued, having composed himself, "this American named Ben falls in love with the Enlightenment Movement and gets a meeting with Rousseau. They become into-the-wee-small-hours-of-the-morning buddies. Rousseau passes the Verities on to Ben, and Ben heads back to the States."

Now, Doc really had my interest. Was he talking about Ben Franklin?

"So, Ben gets through the Verities and starts doing great things, but thinks the 13 Riches should be reversed."

"I don't know what you mean," I said.

"Ben was a tad portly, so the story goes. Instead of focusing only on health, he picks a quality that needs to be executed correctly to shed a few pounds, temperance. So Ben uses the word temperance, instead of sound health," Doc explained. "Then, he invents what was the original spreadsheet. Smart fella. He drew seven columns, one for each day of the week. Then, he put in thirteen rows, one for each of the riches. Ben's idea was that each time you mess up, you make a black mark next to the word. The idea was to work towards getting no black marks."

So, I asked the obvious, "How do the riches come to you?"

Doc replied, "You already know, right?" I nodded and started to say something, but he answered his own question, "Law of Growth. Just focus on what you are working on for the week, not what you don't want. You simply educe each of the 13 Riches with the Law of Growth, the more you notice it, focus on it, the more it shows up... you know, right?" Doc said, nodding his head up and down ever so slightly.

"Yeah, I understand. Concentration on a single thought, like the magnifying glass metaphor," I said.

"You see what I mean now about Ben reversing it?"

"What you think about grows. So, thinking about what you don't want is really the same thing as thinking about it," I said, catching on.

"Yup. You stick with one treasure at time, just like the Verities. Now that you've got fourteen weeks of using The Law of Growth under your belt, the Riches can be drawn out of you and into manifestation in a week. And they will just keep growing, if you just keep holding the thought," Doc promised.

"So, what happened to Ben?" I asked, even though it wasn't really the question I wanted to ask. *Was it Ben Franklin?* To this day, I don't know why I didn't just ask directly.

"He stayed chubby, never really mastered temperance. Wrong approach, ego, I guess, but he had a ton of success, did great, big things. Great imagination, stubborn, too, from what I've been told. Like I said, he had a bit of an ego, took credit for an accidental thing that changed the world."

"What was that?"

"Well, as the story he goes, he was at the local tavern one night, knocking back a few beers. Anything but temperate that night. He gets home, soaked—it's raining cats and dogs—and figures he'll get romantic with his wife. He starts kissing her neck, and she tells him to 'go fly a kite' and yells as he's heading out, 'and don't forget your key.' So he ties the key on the string ... and that's how Franklin discovered electricity. If his bride had said yes, we'd still be sitting in the dark." At this point, Doc couldn't keep a straight face any longer, just cracking himself up at his own bad joke.

I shoot him my best "bad joke" frown. Doc said, "So the legend goes like this. Franklin gives the Verities and The Map to Wordsworth, who passed them on to a guy named Ralph. Wordsworth told Ralph that the handdrawn spreadsheet was Franklin's idea when they met for their 14- week dinner."

"And did he get Ralph a couple of hotdogs, too?" I joked.

"I don't remember any Verity about being a wise-ass," Doc countered. We both giggled like a couple of kids. Doc continued, "Franklin did, however, pass along a clean copy… sort of. I guess he made some minor changes. Ralph goes nuts and keeps meeting with Wordsworth and does his best to figure out what Franklin added, changed, whatever. He studied Rousseau and got it back to what is believed to be original form."

"Would I know this Ralph guy? Who he was?" I was on the edge of my seat, no longer hesitating.

"Emerson. Ralph Waldo Emerson," Doc said nonchalantly. "Ever read his essay, 'The Law of Compensation'? Most critics tend to believe it's as great an essay as has ever been written. It would be hard to read that knowing Verity One and not see the connection."

"So, let me get this straight, Doc. The lynchpin in the Enlightenment Movement had it, passed it to Ben Franklin, and, then, it moved from Wordsworth to Emerson? That's some history of brainpower, great people."

"Yeah, I know. And the women it has passed through are even more impressive, Mark. An outstanding group of greatness."

Of course, I asked about whom some of them were. Doc gazed out at the giraffes for a while, not too long. "Does it matter? I mean, think about it, does it really matter?"

We both fixated on the giraffes for a while. "No," I said, "It doesn't really matter."

"And why not?" Doc prompted, grinning.

"The way I see it, Standing Tall is about character growth, enlightenment of our initial intention. I just don't think the truly enlightened feel like they are better or less than anyone. It really doesn't matter who has had the Verities. The achievements of others or who has had them doesn't make the truth I've discovered more true or less true," I said. "I've heard enough success stories in my lifetime; it's time to create my own."

"Keep going, man," he urged.

"What I know is that the person who is going to change my life is me." I hadn't said it before, but there it was. And it felt right. Check that, I knew it was right as soon as I heard it.

Doc stood up and signaled me with a small hand gesture to stand. He hugged me. Tightly. For a long time. "Well, that's the legend, and there have been a lot of stories about the passing of the Verities. Emerson's best friend was Thoreau. I've read all those guys and either they all understood what you and I have discovered, the primal power of being, or the legend has merit. Either way, no matter because truly you have found the treasure, Mark."

"So you read all those guys?" I asked.

Doc nodded. "Anything you want to know about 'The Map to the 13 Riches'?"

The Mirages

"Yes, in fact, I do want to know something," I replied, as Doc kept a watchful eye on Joey. "What did you ask Toni and Peter about? What did you want to know?"

"I wanted to know about the effortless acquisition of wealth and the mirage metaphor," he said, without hesitation.

I told Doc I didn't really know what they shared with him about those two things, but I did want to know how it worked out for him, what had he experienced.

"We're intended to grow, like all things in nature. It gets effortless, eventually, but for me, it was not effortless at the beginning. What I figured out ,or, should I say, what finally sunk in, was that infinite wealth in the things that really matter is found only in the finite. That was the hard part for me, getting finite." Doc told me that it was all about concentration. "The Law of Growth is going to yield wealth in precise correlation to concentration".

Navigating The Map, for him, was difficult at first. "I still had some garbage in my head. See, I think when average people, like me, get The Verities, they are still thinking about stuff, getting stuff, ya know? Big paycheck, big house, and such… most people have a pretty distorted idea about wealth. I sure did. We've been conditioned to believe that objects and possessions indicate power. We think material success is the most important thing, and that possessions give us power. But, for most of us, they are really symbols of power." He paused, shaking his head. "What a dope. They are just mirages."

"That word stuck with me when I read it, too, Doc."

"There is nothing wrong with owning things, just our perception of what it means. The idea that things give us power or security is dumb. It's a

91

mirage. They won't make you happy, and they don't give you power," Doc said, becoming increasingly animated. "Getting control over your thoughts, there's the wealth. Once you have that, those symbols become confirmations of our power, not power, itself."

The Map

"Letting go of the world's values was the hard part", Doc recalled. "Once I finally did let go, about three or four weeks into The Map, it got effortless. Up until then, I was fighting it a little… old values die hard," he smiled. "I was seeing evidence, the real message of The Verities kicked in, and I got it."

"Got what?" I asked.

"Concentration, the Law of Growth. The Verities set up that great environment in my mind and, week by week, the thing I had focused on, the thing The Map had me focus on, started showing up more and more." He looked out at the giraffes for a while, then, he turned and said, "Peter and Toni just told me to follow the directions on The Map, have my own experience, and enjoy it." Doc put his arm around my neck as he said, "Have your own experience, not mine or theirs. Living vicariously through others— movie stars, ball players, and so forth—robs us of living life. And I'm sure if you were going to live vicariously through someone, it wouldn't be me."
"I get it. Then what?"

"Well, you'll know. Or are you talking about you and I, Mark?" "You and I, Doc."

"Funny thing… I was looking at the Red Sox schedule, and they are playing in Seattle thirteen weeks from this coming Friday. Have you ever been to Seattle?" he asked.

"No, I haven't."

"How about we meet in Seattle at noon on Friday in thirteen weeks. I'll get tickets for games on Friday and Saturday, on me," Doc suggested.

"Gonna' buy me more hot dogs?" I asked, in my best wiseass voice. He got a kick out of it. "Where do you want to meet?"

Doc tipped his chin down, looking over the top of his sunglasses. "You're a smart fella, Mark, and you can figure it out." He was right; I knew where I'd find him at noon in thirteen weeks.

"And we'll go to the ballpark from there," he said. "I'll be anxious to hear about your wealth." And, with that, all conversation ended about The

Verities and The Map, with one exception. "Maps tend to be great if you follow the directions, not so great if you just look at them."

"Fourth Verity?" I asked. He winked.

And, so, we parted for the next thirteen weeks.

Did the wealth happen, you ask? It poured in and keeps pouring in. To make a long story short, after the Map, I have been doing what I love, getting paid great bucks, more than I could have ever imagined, and living on Kauai. It really is paradise for me.

Oh, sure, life has had a few curveballs, challenges, and surprises, but, when you've got The Map, you know what the truly wealthy do… there is always a way once you know that there is always a way. Of all the wealth, wisdom, and riches The Map yielded, my favorite, the one that causes my knees to buckle daily with attacks of gratitude, is the confidence of knowing that there is always a way. While the wealth is great, living a life without fear has been the most priceless treasure The Map yielded for me.

And what about you? What riches will you treasure most? Why not find out for yourself?

After all, you've got The Map…

The Map to the 13 Riches of Life

The Good News. There is a saying, "well begun is half done." Those, like yourself, who have lived with each Verity for two weeks, made promises and kept them is truly one that is well begun and half done. You have been given the tools you shall need to mine the 13 Riches.

The Better News. You are now Standing Tall in character and undoubtedly, like those who have come before you, elevated your values, feeling wealthy in new ways you had not considered previously.

The Best News. A map is merely a depiction of a territory. To successfully move from where one currently is to where one would like to go, we must successfully navigate the terrain, not just look at The Map. The habits of the treasure hunter will determine the outcome, not The Map. The best news for you who now hold The Map is the mental habits needed to successfully navigate, find and claim the 13 Riches of Life have already been established and mastered! No one has ever failed to claim all 13 Riches who has been faithful to the promises made within each Verity. Why settle for The Map when you can have the territory?

The Secret of The Map

There was once a merchant from Egypt traveling with his goods deep into Africa. He was many weeks from his home and thinking of his children after a very long day of work. As he began to head to a lodge to eat and sleep he noticed some young children about the same age as his children playing near the edge of the road. The merchant noticed that the children were playing a game similar to the games his children played with marbles. As he continued to watch them playing his eyes became increasingly more attracted to the small pebbles they were playing with and his heart began to race...

He asked to meet their father. He asked their father about the stones and the father told him "oh, yes, I have more in the hut", and promptly brought out a bowl of the stones. The traveler offered him some cotton and two scarfs for the stones... the Father of the boys laughed, saying "I'm robbing you but if you insist, here you go."

This trade led to the discovery of the largest field of rubies in the world. The fate of the father is really the fate of most human beings. All men and all women hold a fabulous treasure in their possession yet in most cases they just do not know it. We fail to look within for the riches, greater than precious gems. The real treasure in this story is consciousness. The father of the boys did not have the consciousness to understand the riches of the rubies, the traveler did. But there is more to understand so you easily acquire the 13 Riches and the 13 Riches continue to grow in your life in quantities and value beyond your imagination.

Once our traveler made the swap he had to take action to mine them from the ground and transform them into marvelous jewels.
To have wealth beyond measure, you need to emulate this success pattern. It is two simple steps.

Step One is to acknowledge that each of the riches are already in your consciousness, already within you. Step Two, like our traveler, is to mine this wealth.

How does one mine the wealth, the 13 Riches? Using the irrefutable Law of Growth.

What we think about grows. You will recognize each of The 13 Riches and that means they are already in you. We educe each of the 13 Riches, one at a time by applying the Law of Growth. As we go about our day we

95

identify one of the 13 Riches everywhere, in everyone and in everything. As the week progresses, because you are building a consciousness for it, you will draw out of yourself, in greater quantities everyday. That which we identify, tends to multiply. The more often you find what you are concentrating on for that day, the more it will grow to an overflowing experience. By weeks end, for each of the 13 Riches, you will be astonished by the abundance of each.

You have begun to be a master of The Law of Growth during the last 14 weeks and all you must do now is follow The Map, one day at a time, as you followed the Verities. Read, promise and execute ... and to accelerate your wealth, keep sharing it as the grateful giver you are.

The First of the 13 Riches
A Positive Mental Attitude

You already have a beautiful start on a positive mental attitude. Draw this treasure out by following the directions on the map for the next seven days. All the other riches on the map are easy to find and effortless to claim for those with a positive mental attitude.

A positive mental attitude is the first of the 13 Riches. The Law of Environment, simply stated, is that the things that belong in that environment must show up and will quickly flourish. A positive mental attitude sets the best possible environment to grow the riches. Success has requirements. The Law of Growth and the Law of Environment are the little hinges that swing open the big doors of wealth in all areas of life. When we have a positive mental attitude, the environment within our mind, good things, the riches, grow faster. One cannot be positive twenty to thirty minutes a day while reading and taking time to think then be negative the rest of the day and expect positive riches to grow. What we think about grows and it takes far less effort to grow riches that are in a positive environment. The other 12 Riches will quickly bloom and multiply for those with a positive mental environment. A positive mental environment is a by-product of positive mental attitude that has been defined, refined and mastered.

Day One

Growing My Wealth With A Positive Mental Attitude

Read this out loud when you arise; from "I promise to" through "I always keep my promises". Be certain to sign it and include your name in the reading out loud.

I promise to follow these 3 steps today

1. I read the First Verity two times today, first thing in the morning and aloud in the evening just before I go to bed.
2. I read my "Intention" card three times today with enthusiasm.
3. As I go through my day, I identify every example of a positive mental attitude.

_____

I always keep my promises

Here are a few examples of a positive mental attitude. Compliments, hugs, handshakes, people sharing with you good things they are anticipating, smiling... Note each one and check off a box for each example you find during the day. Find some of your own! See the best in everything, everywhere and everyone. The more you identify the more you will grow this priceless gift that is latent within you.

○ ○ ○ ○ ○   ○ ○ ○ ○ ○   ○ ○ ○ ○ ○   ○ ○ ○ ○ ○   ○ ○ ○ ○ ○

Before your nighttime read and sitting still, check off the examples you saw. Each day the number you spot will grow if you focus.

Jot down the best example you observed today of a positive mental attitude.

Day Two
Growing My Wealth With A Positive Mental Attitude

Read this out loud when you arise; from "I promise to" through "I always keep my promises". Be certain to sign it and include your name in the reading out loud.

I promise to follow these 3 steps today

1. I read the First Verity two times today, first thing in the morning and aloud in the evening just before I go to bed.
2. I read my "Intention" card three times today with enthusiasm.
3. As I go through my day, I identify every example of a positive mental attitude

_____

I always keep my promises

Here are a few examples of a positive mental attitude. Compliments, hugs, hand shakes, people sharing with you good things they are anticipating, smiling... Note each one and check off a box for each example you find during the day. Find some of your own! See the best in everything, everywhere and everyone. The more you identify the more you will grow this priceless gift that is latent within you.

○○○○○ ○○○○○ ○○○○○ ○○○○○ ○○○○○

Before your nighttime read and sitting still, check off the examples you saw. Each day the number you spot will grow if you focus.
Jot down the best example you observed today of a positive mental attitude.

Day Three
Growing My Wealth With A Positive Mental Attitude

Read this out loud when you arise; from "I promise to" through "I always keep my promises". Be certain to sign it and include your name in the reading out loud.

I promise to follow these 3 steps today

1. I read the First Verity two times today, first thing in the morning and aloud in the evening just before I go to bed.
2. I read my "Intention" card three times today with enthusiasm.
3. As I go through my day, I identify every example of a positive mental attitude.

_____

I always keep my promises

Here are a few examples of a positive mental attitude. Compliments, hugs, handshakes, people sharing with you good things they are anticipating, smiling... Note each one and check off a box for each example you find during the day. Find some of your own! See the best in everything, everywhere and everyone. The more you identify the more you will grow this priceless gift that is latent within you.

○○○○○ ○○○○○ ○○○○○ ○○○○○ ○○○○○

Before your nighttime read and sitting still, check off the examples you saw. Each day the number you spot will grow if you focus.
Jot down the best example you observed today of a positive mental attitude.

100

Day Four
Growing My Wealth With A Positive Mental Attitude

Read this out loud when you arise; from "I promise to" through "I always keep my promises". Be certain to sign it and include your name in the reading out loud.

I promise to follow these 3 steps today
1. I read the First Verity two times today, first thing in the morning and aloud in the evening just before I go to bed.
2. I read my "Intention" card three times today with enthusiasm.
3. As I go through my day, I identify every example of a positive mental attitude.

_____

I always keep my promises

Here are a few examples of a positive mental attitude. Compliments, hugs, handshakes, people sharing with you good things they are anticipating, smiling... Note each one and check off a box for each example you find during the day. Find some of your own! See the best in everything, everywhere and everyone. The more you identify the more you will grow this priceless gift that is latent within you.

○○○○○ ○○○○○ ○○○○○ ○○○○○ ○○○○○

Before your nighttime read and sitting still, check off the examples you saw. Each day the number you spot will grow if you focus.
Jot down the best example you observed today of a positive mental attitude.

Day Five
Growing My Wealth With A Positive Mental Attitude

Read this out loud when you arise; from "I promise to" through "I always keep my promises". Be certain to sign it and include your name in the reading out loud.

I promise to follow these 3 steps today
1. I read the First Verity two times today, first thing in the morning and aloud in the evening just before I go to bed.
2. I read my "Intention" card three times today with enthusiasm.
3. As I go through my day, I identify every example of a positive mental attitude.

_____

I always keep my promises

Here are a few examples of a positive mental attitude. Compliments, hugs, handshakes, people sharing with you good things they are anticipating, smiling... Note each one and check off a box for each example you find during the day. Find some of your own! See the best in everything, everywhere and everyone. The more you identify the more you will grow this priceless gift that is latent within you.

○○○○○　○○○○○　○○○○○　○○○○○　○○○○○

Before your nighttime read and sitting still, check off the examples you saw. Each day the number you spot will grow if you focus.

Jot down the best example you observed today of a positive mental attitude.

Day Six
Growing My Wealth With A Positive Mental Attitude

Read this out loud when you arise; from "I promise to" through "I always keep my promises". Be certain to sign it and include your name in the reading out loud.

I promise to follow these 3 steps today
1. I read the First Verity two times today, first thing in the morning and aloud in the evening just before I go to bed.
2. I read my "Intention" card three times today with enthusiasm.
3. As I go through my day, I identify every example of a positive mental attitude.

_____

I always keep my promises

Here are a few examples of a positive mental attitude. Compliments, hugs, handshakes, people sharing with you good things they are anticipating, smiling... Note each one and check off a box for each example you find during the day. Find some of your own! See the best in everything, everywhere and everyone. The more you identify the more you will grow this priceless gift that is latent within you.

○ ○ ○ ○ ○   ○ ○ ○ ○ ○   ○ ○ ○ ○ ○   ○ ○ ○ ○ ○   ○ ○ ○ ○ ○

Before your nighttime read and sitting still, check off the examples you saw. Each day the number you spot will grow if you focus.
Jot down the best example you observed today of a positive mental attitude.

Day Seven

Growing My Wealth With A Positive Mental Attitude

Read this out loud when you arise; from "I promise to" through "I always keep my promises". Be certain to sign it and include your name in the reading out loud.

I promise to follow these 3 steps today

1. I read the First Verity two times today, first thing in the morning and aloud in the evening just before I go to bed.
2. I read my "Intention" card three times today with enthusiasm.
3. As I go through my day, I identify every example of a positive mental attitude.

_____

I always keep my promises

Here are a few examples of a positive mental attitude. Compliments, hugs, handshakes, people sharing with you good things they are anticipating, smiling... Note each one and check off a box for each example you find during the day. Find some of your own! See the best in everything, everywhere and everyone. The more you identify the more you will grow this priceless gift that is latent within you.

○○○○○ ○○○○○ ○○○○○ ○○○○○ ○○○○○

Before your nighttime read and sitting still, check off the examples you saw. Each day the number you spot will grow if you focus.

Jot down the best example you observed today of a positive mental attitude.

The Second of the 13 Riches
Sound Physical Health

To Stand Taller, to embrace more out of our relationships, our potential and our work, we must make certain that the body is of sound physical health. Sound Physical Health today and gratitude for it are imperative to wealth in all areas of your life. The best navigators of The Map had the physical fitness and were able to find the place where even more wealth is available. Where is that place? The extra mile. While most people don't appreciate their health until it is impeded, Masters of the Verities live in a state of gratitude for their health each day.

Day One (Week 2)
Growing My Wealth With Sound Physical Health

Read this out loud when you arise; from "I promise to" through "I always keep my promises". Be certain to sign it and include your name in the reading out loud.

I promise to follow these 4 steps today

1. I read the Second Verity two times today, first thing in the morning and aloud in the evening just before I go to bed.
2. I read my "Intention" card three times today with enthusiasm.
3. I affirm with vigor, "I feel healthy, I feel happy, I feel terrific!" 10 times and when any one asks me how I am or how I am doing, that affirmation is always the answer I give with great conviction.
4. As I go through my day, I identify Sound Physical Health choices constantly.

_____

I always keep my promises

Here are a few examples of acts that foster Sound Physical Health. Exercise, healthy choices others make with food, people healing, people who help others heal. Note each one and check off a box for each example you find during the day. Find some of your own! The more you identify the more you will grow this priceless gift that is latent within you.

O O O O O   O O O O O   O O O O O   O O O O O   O O O O O

Before your nighttime read and sitting still, check off the examples you saw. Each day the number you spot will grow if you focus.

Jot down the best example you observed of Sound Physical Health today.

106

Day Two (Week 2)
Growing My Wealth With Sound Physical Health

Read this out loud when you arise; from "I promise to" through "I always keep my promises". Be certain to sign it and include your name in the reading out loud.

I promise to follow these 4 steps today

1. I read the Second Verity two times today, first thing in the morning and aloud in the evening just before I go to bed.
2. I read my "Intention" card three times today with enthusiasm.
3. I affirm with vigor, "I feel healthy, I feel happy, I feel terrific!" 10 times and when any one asks me how I am or how I am doing, that affirmation is always the answer I give with great conviction.
4. As I go through my day, I identify Sound Physical Health choices constantly.

_____

I always keep my promises

Here are a few examples of acts that foster Sound Physical Health. Exercise, healthy choices others make with food, people healing, people who help others heal. Note each one and check off a box for each example you find during the day. Find some of your own! The more you identify the more you will grow this priceless gift that is latent within you.

○○○○○ ○○○○○ ○○○○○ ○○○○○ ○○○○○

Before your nighttime read and sitting still, check off the examples you saw. Each day the number you spot will grow if you focus.
Jot down the best example you observed of Sound Physical Health today.

107

Day Three (Week 2)
Growing My Wealth With Sound Physical Health

Read this out loud when you arise; from "I promise to" through "I always keep my promises". Be certain to sign it and include your name in the reading out loud.

I promise to follow these 4 steps today

1. I read the Second Verity two times today, first thing in the morning and aloud in the evening just before I go to bed.
2. I read my "Intention" card three times today with enthusiasm.
3. I affirm with vigor, "I feel healthy, I feel happy, I feel terrific!" 10 times and when any one asks me how I am or how I am doing, that affirmation is always the answer I give with great conviction.
4. As I go through my day, I identify Sound Physical Health choices constantly.

_____

I always keep my promises

Here are a few examples of acts that foster Sound Physical Health. Exercise, healthy choices others make with food, people healing, people who help others heal. Note each one and check off a box for each example you find during the day. Find some of your own! The more you identify the more you will grow this priceless gift that is latent within you.

○○○○○　○○○○○　○○○○○　○○○○○　○○○○○

Before your nighttime read and sitting still, check off the examples you saw. Each day the number you spot will grow if you focus.
Jot down the best example you observed of Sound Physical Health today.

108

Day Four (Week 2)
Growing My Wealth With Sound Physical Health

Read this out loud when you arise; from "I promise to" through "I always keep my promises". Be certain to sign it and include your name in the reading out loud.

I promise to follow these 4 steps today
1. I read the Second Verity two times today, first thing in the morning and aloud in the evening just before I go to bed.
2. I read my "Intention" card three times today with enthusiasm.
3. I affirm with vigor, "I feel healthy, I feel happy, I feel terrific!" 10 times and when any one asks me how I am or how I am doing, that affirmation is always the answer I give with great conviction.
4. As I go through my day, I identify Sound Physical Health choices constantly.

_____

I always keep my promises

Here are a few examples of acts that foster Sound Physical Health. Exercise, healthy choices others make with food, people healing, people who help others heal. Note each one and check off a box for each example you find during the day. Find some of your own! The more you identify the more you will grow this priceless gift that is latent within you.

○○○○○ ○○○○○ ○○○○○ ○○○○○ ○○○○○

Before your nighttime read and sitting still, check off the examples you saw. Each day the number you spot will grow if you focus.
Jot down the best example you observed of Sound Physical Health today.

Day Five (Week 2)
Growing My Wealth With Sound Physical Health

Read this out loud when you arise; from "I promise to" through "I always keep my promises". Be certain to sign it and include your name in the reading out loud.

I promise to follow these 4 steps today

1. I read the Second Verity two times today, first thing in the morning and aloud in the evening just before I go to bed.
2. I read my "Intention" card three times today with enthusiasm.
3. I affirm with vigor, "I feel healthy, I feel happy, I feel terrific!" 10 times and when any one asks me how I am or how I am doing, that affirmation is always the answer I give with great conviction.
4. As I go through my day, I identify Sound Physical Health choices constantly.

_____

I always keep my promises

Here are a few examples of acts that foster Sound Physical Health. Exercise, healthy choices others make with food, people healing, people who help others heal. Note each one and check off a box for each example you find during the day. Find some of your own! The more you identify the more you will grow this priceless gift that is latent within you.

○○○○○   ○○○○○   ○○○○○   ○○○○○   ○○○○○

Before your nighttime read and sitting still, check off the examples you saw. Each day the number you spot will grow if you focus.
Jot down the best example you observed of Sound Physical Health today.

Day Six (Week 2)
Growing My Wealth With Sound Physical Health

Read this out loud when you arise; from "I promise to" through "I always keep my promises". Be certain to sign it and include your name in the reading out loud.

I promise to follow these 4 steps today

I read the Second Verity two times today, first thing in the morning and aloud in the evening just before I go to bed.

I read my "Intention" card three times today with enthusiasm.

I affirm with vigor, "I feel healthy, I feel happy, I feel terrific!" 10 times and when any one asks me how I am or how I am doing, that affirmation is always the answer I give with great conviction.

As I go through my day, I identify Sound Physical Health choices constantly.

———————————————————

I always keep my promises

Here are a few examples of acts that foster Sound Physical Health. Exercise, healthy choices others make with food, people healing, people who help others heal. Note each one and check off a box for each example you find during the day. Find some of your own! The more you identify the more you will grow this priceless gift that is latent within you.

O O O O O   O O O O O   O O O O O   O O O O O   O O O O O

Before your nighttime read and sitting still, check off the examples you saw. Each day the number you spot will grow if you focus.

Jot down the best example you observed of Sound Physical Health today.

Day Seven (Week 2)
Growing My Wealth With Sound Physical Health

Read this out loud when you arise; from "I promise to" through "I always keep my promises". Be certain to sign it and include your name in the reading out loud.

I promise to follow these 4 steps today

1. I read the Second Verity two times today, first thing in the morning and aloud in the evening just before I go to bed.
2. I read my "Intention" card three times today with enthusiasm.
3. I affirm with vigor, "I feel healthy, I feel happy, I feel terrific!" 10 times and when any one asks me how I am or how I am doing, that affirmation is always the answer I give with great conviction.
4. As I go through my day, I identify Sound Physical Health choices constantly.

_____

I always keep my promises

Here are a few examples of acts that foster Sound Physical Health. Exercise, healthy choices others make with food, people healing, people who help others heal. Note each one and check off a box for each example you find during the day. Find some of your own! The more you identify the more you will grow this priceless gift that is latent within you.

O O O O O   O O O O O   O O O O O   O O O O O   O O O O O

Before your nighttime read and sitting still, check off the examples you saw. Each day the number you spot will grow if you focus.
Jot down the best example you observed of Sound Physical Health today.

The Third of the 13 Riches
An Open Mind

You have a tremendous head start on open-mindedness because of your introduction to and practice of detachment. Attachment to the past is what closes our mind. Part of our past is the sense of self, our beliefs. To penetrate new worlds, to discover new ideas, to unearth better and faster ways to manifest our intention and to open up to the possibility that our intention is more powerful and grand than when first conceived, we must stay open to everything and be attached to nothing.

This means, from time to time, to accept a better way we must let a belief system go. To the untrained eye a seed appears to be in a state of destruction when it's shell breaks away, its insides come out and all it was changes. Yet it is this apparent destruction that yields new life, growth and wonder... A seed, held in a hand, has no value because it cannot become what it was intended to be. Only when it is dropped into the soil and self-destructs its shell does the miracle of infinite grow happen. For as the plant grows, it brings with it more seeds that when released create even more plants. In turn, with those plants come more seeds and they produce fields that eventually produce acres ... and there is no end to this effect.

See the soil as the world of infinite possibilities and the shell as attachment. Your willingness to stay open-minded is like the hand that releases the seed to the soil. And, like that seed, you will discover there is no end to the growth of those who remain open-minded.

Day One (Week 3)
Growing My Wealth With An Open Mind

Read this out loud when you arise; from "I promise to" through "I always keep my promises". Be certain to sign it and include your name in the reading out loud.

I promise to follow these 3 steps today

1. *I read the Third Verity two times today, first thing in the morning and aloud in the evening just before I go to bed.*
2. *I read my "Intention" card three times today with enthusiasm*
3. *As I go through my day, I identify every example of open-mindedness.*

_____

I always keep my promises

Here are a few examples of open-mindedness. Listening, nodding, agreements, asking questions, fascination, trying different foods, beverages... Note each one and check off a box for each example you find during the day. Find some of your own! The more you identify the more open your mind will become and a rich flow of ideas will flow unto to you in great quantities daily.

○○○○○ ○○○○○ ○○○○○ ○○○○○ ○○○○○

Before your nighttime read and sitting still, check off the examples you saw. Each day the number you spot will grow if you focus.
Jot down the best example you observed today of open-mindedness.

Day Two (Week 3)
Growing My Wealth With An Open Mind

Read this out loud when you arise; from "I promise to" through "I always keep my promises". Be certain to sign it and include your name in the reading out loud.

I promise to follow these 3 steps today

1. I read the Third Verity two times today, first thing in the morning and aloud in the evening just before I go to bed.
2. I read my "Intention" card three times today with enthusiasm
3. As I go through my day, I identify every example of open-mindedness.

_____

I always keep my promises

Here are a few examples of open-mindedness. Listening, nodding, agreements, asking questions, fascination, trying different foods, beverages... Note each one and check off a box for each example you find during the day. Find some of your own! The more you identify the more open your mind will become and a rich flow of ideas will flow unto to you in great quantities daily.

○ ○ ○ ○ ○   ○ ○ ○ ○ ○   ○ ○ ○ ○ ○   ○ ○ ○ ○ ○   ○ ○ ○ ○ ○

Before your nighttime read and sitting still, check off the examples you saw. Each day the number you spot will grow if you focus.
Jot down the best example you observed today of open-mindedness.

Day Three (Week 3)
Growing My Wealth With An Open Mind

Read this out loud when you arise; from "I promise to" through "I always keep my promises". Be certain to sign it and include your name in the reading out loud.

I promise to follow these 3 steps today

1. I read the Third Verity two times today, first thing in the morning and aloud in the evening just before I go to bed.
2. I read my "Intention" card three times today with enthusiasm
3. As I go through my day, I identify every example of open-mindedness.

_____

I always keep my promises

Here are a few examples of open-mindedness. Listening, nodding, agreements, asking questions, fascination, trying different foods, beverages... Note each one and check off a box for each example you find during the day. Find some of your own! The more you identify the more open your mind will become and a rich flow of ideas will flow unto to you in great quantities daily.

○○○○○　○○○○○　○○○○○　○○○○○　○○○○○

Before your nighttime read and sitting still, check off the examples you saw. Each day the number you spot will grow if you focus.
Jot down the best example you observed today of open-mindedness.

Day Four (Week 3)
Growing My Wealth With An Open Mind

Read this out loud when you arise; from "I promise to" through "I always keep my promises". Be certain to sign it and include your name in the reading out loud.

I promise to follow these 3 steps today

1. *I read the Third Verity two times today, first thing in the morning and aloud in the evening just before I go to bed.*
2. *I read my "Intention" card three times today with enthusiasm*
3. *As I go through my day, I identify every example of open-mindedness.*

_____

I always keep my promises

Here are a few examples of open-mindedness. Listening, nodding, agreements, asking questions, fascination, trying different foods, beverages... Note each one and check off a box for each example you find during the day. Find some of your own! The more you identify the more open your mind will become and a rich flow of ideas will flow unto to you in great quantities daily.

O O O O O O O O O O O O O O O O O O O O O O O O O

Before your nighttime read and sitting still, check off the examples you saw. Each day the number you spot will grow if you focus.
Jot down the best example you observed today of open-mindedness.

117

Day Five (Week 3)
Growing My Wealth With An Open Mind

Read this out loud when you arise; from "I promise to" through "I always keep my promises". Be certain to sign it and include your name in the reading out loud.

I promise to follow these 3 steps today

1. I read the Third Verity two times today, first thing in the morning and aloud in the evening just before I go to bed.
2. I read my "Intention" card three times today with enthusiasm
3. As I go through my day, I identify every example of open-mindedness.

_____

I always keep my promises

Here are a few examples of open-mindedness. Listening, nodding, agreements, asking questions, fascination, trying different foods, beverages... Note each one and check off a box for each example you find during the day. Find some of your own! The more you identify the more open your mind will become and a rich flow of ideas will flow unto to you in great quantities daily.

O O O O O   O O O O O   O O O O O   O O O O O   O O O O O

Before your nighttime read and sitting still, check off the examples you saw. Each day the number you spot will grow if you focus.
Jot down the best example you observed today of open-mindedness.

Day Six (Week 3)
Growing My Wealth With An Open Mind

Read this out loud when you arise; from "I promise to" through "I always keep my promises". Be certain to sign it and include your name in the reading out loud.

I promise to follow these 3 steps today
1. I read the Third Verity two times today, first thing in the morning and aloud in the evening just before I go to bed.
2. I read my "Intention" card three times today with enthusiasm
3. As I go through my day, I identify every example of open-mindedness.

_____

I always keep my promises

Here are a few examples of open-mindedness. Listening, nodding, agreements, asking questions, fascination, trying different foods, beverages... Note each one and check off a box for each example you find during the day. Find some of your own! The more you identify the more open your mind will become and a rich flow of ideas will flow unto to you in great quantities daily.

OOOOO OOOOO OOOOO OOOOO OOOOO

Before your nighttime read and sitting still, check off the examples you saw. Each day the number you spot will grow if you focus.
Jot down the best example you observed today of open-mindedness.

Day Seven (Week 3)
Growing My Wealth With An Open Mind

Read this out loud when you arise; from "I promise to" through "I always keep my promises". Be certain to sign it and include your name in the reading out loud.

I promise to follow these 3 steps today
1. I read the Third Verity two times today, first thing in the morning and aloud in the evening just before I go to bed.
2. I read my "Intention" card three times today with enthusiasm
3. As I go through my day, I identify every example of open-mindedness.

_____

I always keep my promises

Here are a few examples of open-mindedness. Listening, nodding, agreements, asking questions, fascination, trying different foods, beverages... Note each one and check off a box for each example you find during the day. Find some of your own! The more you identify the more open your mind will become and a rich flow of ideas will flow unto to you in great quantities daily.

○○○○○　○○○○○　○○○○○　○○○○○　○○○○○

Before your nighttime read and sitting still, check off the examples you saw. Each day the number you spot will grow if you focus.
Jot down the best example you observed today of open-mindedness.

120

The Fourth of the 13 Riches
The Capacity to Direct Faith

Faith is essential in manifesting your intention. The great navigators of the Map to the 13 Riches in Life share a remarkable insight that forges wealth beyond imagination and becomes bewildering. While most people see faith as a mystical force, very few have discovered what it actually is and how to use it. And with thousands of definitions already written and undoubtedly many thousands to be written, take great care to absorb this simple truth. Everyone, meaning all people, have equal faith. It is not a question of "having faith" but simply a question of "directing" it towards the things you desire to manifest. This is known to the wealthy as equal faith.

Horatio looks at Desdemona and says to his friend Julius, "Desdemona has great faith, and I wish I had as much faith as she does." Horatio has the same, exact amount of faith as Desdemona; he has just directed his faith, what he actually believes, at the thought that he does not have as much faith as Desdemona. He has placed his faith in doubt and believes that just as faithfully as the thing he perceives Desdemona has faith in. Faith, in essence, is belief. Since our beliefs are by-products of thoughts charged with feeling and we have control over our thoughts, we have total control over our faith.

Celebrate the truth! Your creator did not decide to give Horatio 50% of the faith he gave to Desdemona or to you. You have been given control over one thing; thought. Since faith is a by-product of our thoughts and you have the capacity to control your thoughts you also have the capacity to direct your faith. You need never struggle with doubt again and this makes you wealthy for that which we create in thought and believe must manifest provided it is good for you, takes no one else's good and is in harmony with The Source.

121

Day One (Week 4)
Growing My Wealth By Directing My Faith

Read this out loud when you arise; from "I promise to" through "I always keep my promises". Be certain to sign it and include your name in the reading out loud.

I promise to follow these 3 steps today
1. *I read the Fourth Verity two times today, first thing in the morning and aloud in the evening just before I go to bed.*
2. *I read my "Intention" card three times today with enthusiasm*
3. *As I go through my day, I identify acts of faith*

I always keep my promises

Here are a few examples of acts of faith. Confident speech, hope, anticipation, predictions, projections, goals, people frequenting merchants, kind words about people not present, places of worship... Note each one and check off a box for each example you find during the day. Find some of your own! The more you identify acts of faith the more control you will have over directing your own. Directed faith at your intention leads to faster manifestation because human thoughts have a tendency to express themselves on the physical plane when charged with directed faith..

○○○○○ ○○○○○ ○○○○○ ○○○○○ ○○○○○

Before your nighttime read and sitting still, check off the examples you saw. Each day the number you spot will grow if you focus.
Jot down the best example you observed today of faith.

122

Day Two (Week 4)
Growing My Wealth By Directing My Faith

Read this out loud when you arise; from "I promise to" through "I always keep my promises". Be certain to sign it and include your name in the reading out loud.

I promise to follow these 3 steps today

1. *I read the Fourth Verity two times today, first thing in the morning and aloud in the evening just before I go to bed.*
2. *I read my "Intention" card three times today with enthusiasm*
3. *As I go through my day, I identify acts of faith*

I always keep my promises　　　

Here are a few examples of acts of faith. Confident speech, hope, anticipation, predictions, projections, goals, people frequenting merchants, kind words about people not present, places of worship, a child coming to the dinner table with expectation they'll be feed; note each one and check off a box for each example you find during the day. Find some of your own! The more you identify acts of faith the more control you will have over directing your own. Directed faith at your intention leads to faster manifestation because human thoughts have a tendency to express themselves on the physical plane when charged with directed faith

○○○○○　○○○○○　○○○○○　○○○○○　○○○○○

Before your nighttime read and sitting still, check off the examples you saw. Each day the number you spot will grow if you focus.
Jot down the best example you observed today of faith.

Day Three (Week 4)
Growing My Wealth By Directing My Faith

Read this out loud when you arise; from "I promise to" through "I always keep my promises". Be certain to sign it and include your name in the reading out loud.

I promise to follow these 3 steps today

1. I read the Fourth Verity two times today, first thing in the morning and aloud in the evening just before I go to bed.
2. I read my "Intention" card three times today with enthusiasm
3. As I go through my day, I identify acts of faith

_____

I always keep my promises

Here are a few examples of acts of faith. Confident speech, hope, anticipation, predictions, projections, goals, people frequenting merchants, kind words about people not present, places of worship… Note each one and check off a box for each example you find during the day. Find some of your own! The more you identify acts of faith the more control you will have over directing your own. Directed faith at your intention leads to faster manifestation because human thoughts have a tendency to express themselves on the physical plane when charged with directed faith.

○○○○○ ○○○○○ ○○○○○ ○○○○○ ○○○○○

Before your nighttime read and sitting still, check off the examples you saw. Each day the number you spot will grow if you focus.
Jot down the best example you observed today of faith.

Day Four (Week 4)
Growing My Wealth By Directing My Faith

Read this out loud when you arise; from "I promise to" through "I always keep my promises". Be certain to sign it and include your name in the reading out loud.

I promise to follow these 3 steps today
1. *I read the Fourth Verity two times today, first thing in the morning and aloud in the evening just before I go to bed.*
2. *I read my "Intention" card three times today with enthusiasm*
3. *As I go through my day, I identify acts of faith*

_____

I always keep my promises

Here are a few examples of acts of faith. Confident speech, hope, anticipation, predictions, projections, goals, people frequenting merchants, kind words about people not present, places of worship... Note each one and check off a box for each example you find during the day. Find some of your own! The more you identify acts of faith the more control you will have over directing your own. Directed faith at your intention leads to faster manifestation because human thoughts have a tendency to express themselves on the physical plane when charged with directed faith.

○○○○○ ○○○○○ ○○○○○ ○○○○○ ○○○○○

Before your nighttime read and sitting still, check off the examples you saw. Each day the number you spot will grow if you focus.
Jot down the best example you observed today of faith.

Day Five (Week 4)
Growing My Wealth By Directing My Faith

Read this out loud when you arise; from "I promise to" through "I always keep my promises". Be certain to sign it and include your name in the reading out loud.

I promise to follow these 3 steps today
1. *I read the Fourth Verity two times today, first thing in the morning and aloud in the evening just before I go to bed.*
2. *I read my "Intention" card three times today with enthusiasm*
3. *As I go through my day, I identify acts of faith*

_____

I always keep my promises

Here are a few examples of acts of faith. Confident speech, hope, anticipation, predictions, projections, goals, people frequenting merchants, kind words about people not present, places of worship... Note each one and check off a box for each example you find during the day. Find some of your own! The more you identify acts of faith the more control you will have over directing your own. Directed faith at your intention leads to faster manifestation because human thoughts have a tendency to express themselves on the physical plane when charged with directed faith.

O O O O O   O O O O O   O O O O O   O O O O O   O O O O O

Before your nighttime read and sitting still, check off the examples you saw. Each day the number you spot will grow if you focus.
Jot down the best example you observed today of faith.

Day Six (Week 4)
Growing My Wealth By Directing My Faith

Read this out loud when you arise; from "I promise to" through "I always keep my promises". Be certain to sign it and include your name in the reading out loud.

I promise to follow these 3 steps today
1. I read the Fourth Verity two times today, first thing in the morning and aloud in the evening just before I go to bed.
2. I read my "Intention" card three times today with enthusiasm
3. As I go through my day, I identify acts of faith

_____

I always keep my promises

Here are a few examples of acts of faith. Confident speech, hope, anticipation, predictions, projections, goals, people frequenting merchants, kind words about people not present, places of worship... Note each one and check off a box for each example you find during the day. Find some of your own! The more you identify acts of faith the more control you will have over directing your own. Directed faith at your intention leads to faster manifestation because human thoughts have a tendency to express themselves on the physical plane when charged with directed faith.

○○○○○ ○○○○○ ○○○○○ ○○○○○ ○○○○○

Before your nighttime read and sitting still, check off the examples you saw. Each day the number you spot will grow if you focus.
Jot down the best example you observed today of faith.

Day Seven (Week 4)
Growing My Wealth By Directing My Faith

Read this out loud when you arise; from "I promise to" through "I always keep my promises". Be certain to sign it and include your name in the reading out loud.

I promise to follow these 3 steps today
1. I read the Fourth Verity two times today, first thing in the morning and aloud in the evening just before I go to bed.
2. I read my "Intention" card three times today with enthusiasm
3. As I go through my day, I identify acts of faith

_____

I always keep my promises

Here are a few examples of acts of faith. Confident speech, hope, anticipation, predictions, projections, goals, people frequenting merchants, kind words about people not present, places of worship... Note each one and check off a box for each example you find during the day. Find some of your own! The more you identify acts of faith the more control you will have over directing your own. Directed faith at your intention leads to faster manifestation because human thoughts have a tendency to express themselves on the physical plane when charged with directed faith. .

○○○○○ ○○○○○ ○○○○○ ○○○○○ ○○○○○

Before your nighttime read and sitting still, check off the examples you saw. Each day the number you spot will grow if you focus.
Jot down the best example you observed today of faith.

128

The Fifth of the 13 Riches
Liberty

Liberty is living fearlessly. Where does fear come from and what is it, really? As newborn children we have only two fears; fear of loud noises and fear of falling. All other fears are learned. As we go through life, things happen. Those things mean nothing in and of themselves. We make up a story about those things and the stories we make up set the limits and possibilities for ourselves. Another way to phrase this is "perception." Therefore, fear is error in the story we make up, in our perceptions.

Where do these foundations come from that alter our perceptions so we sense fear about an outcome of something that has not happened? Since all fear has no vitality, it cannot survive unless we give it power in thought by staying loyal to the story we made up. Understanding where these foundations come from is essential in eliminating fear. They all are learned behaviors based on other people's opinions and perceptions.

Since we are tribal by nature, wanting to belong to the tribe, we unknowingly seek approval of the tribe. At the very foundation of our fears is conformity to obtain approval and avoid ridicule and rejection. Conformity is what jails liberty and becomes the inhibitor of growth. Imagine your life without fear, how many more things would you experience? There is no price too high to pay for the liberty of owning yourself and being comfortable in your own skin. Living a life absent of self-consciousness is, in a word, priceless.

And what is that price? Respect for all people and loyalty to the person you were intended to become. Those who have claimed the riches of liberty, become comfortable in their own skin, simply let go of what is no longer needed, and summoned the courage to be their authentic self. To know thyself and to be thyself is to experience liberty. What did the great ones do? They knew, as you do, that if their intention was in harmony with The Source that the only other approval they would need was their own.

Day One (Week 5)
Growing My Wealth With Liberty

Read this out loud when you arise; from "I promise to" through "I always keep my promises". Be certain to sign it and include your name in the reading out loud.

I promise to follow these 3 steps today
1. *I read the Fifth Verity two times today, first thing in the morning and aloud in the evening just before I go to bed.*
2. *I read my "Intention" card three times today with enthusiasm*
3. *As I go through my day, I identify liberty with magnifying glass focus all day*

_____

I always keep my promises

Here are a few examples of acts of liberty. Children being themselves, people who make their requests clear, pets, non-self conscious behavior, people making fun of themselves, confidence, people taking risks, encouragement, all animals... Note each one and check off a box for each example you find during the day. Find some of your own! The more you identify liberty the more liberty you will experience. Look for it everywhere and use the immutable Law of Growth to grow it within your heart.

○○○○○　○○○○○　○○○○○　○○○○○　○○○○○

Before your nighttime read and sitting still, check off the examples you saw. Each day the number you spot will grow if you focus.
Jot down the best example you observed today of liberty.

131

Day Two (Week 5)
Growing My Wealth With Liberty

Read this out loud when you arise; from "I promise to" through "I always keep my promises". Be certain to sign it and include your name in the reading out loud.

I promise to follow these 3 steps today

1. I read the Fifth Verity two times today, first thing in the morning and aloud in the evening just before I go to bed.
2. I read my "Intention" card three times today with enthusiasm
3. As I go through my day, I identify liberty with magnifying glass focus all day

_____

I always keep my promises

Here are a few examples of acts of liberty. Children being themselves, people who make their requests clear, pets, non-self conscious behavior, people making fun of themselves, confidence, people taking risks, encouragement, all animals... Note each one and check off a box for each example you find during the day. Find some of your own! The more you identify liberty the more liberty you will experience. Look for it everywhere and use the immutable Law of Growth to grow it within your heart.

○○○○○ ○○○○○ ○○○○○ ○○○○○ ○○○○○

Before your nighttime read and sitting still, check off the examples you saw. Each day the number you spot will grow if you focus.
Jot down the best example you observed today of liberty.

132

Day Three (Week 5)
Growing My Wealth With Liberty

Read this out loud when you arise; from "I promise to" through "I always keep my promises". Be certain to sign it and include your name in the reading out loud.

I promise to follow these 3 steps today
1. I read the Fifth Verity two times today, first thing in the morning and aloud in the evening just before I go to bed.
2. I read my "Intention" card three times today with enthusiasm
3. As I go through my day, I identify liberty with magnifying glass focus all day

_____

I always keep my promises

Here are a few of examples of acts of liberty. Children being themselves, people who make their requests clear, pets, non-self conscious behavior, people making fun of themselves, confidence, people taking risks, encouragement, all animals... Note each one and check off a box for each example you find during the day. Find some of your own! The more you identify liberty the more liberty you will experience. Look for it everywhere and use the immutable Law of Growth to grow it within your heart

○○○○○ ○○○○○ ○○○○○ ○○○○○ ○○○○○

Before your nighttime read and sitting still, check off the examples you saw. Each day the number you spot will grow if you focus.
Jot down the best example you observed today of liberty.

Day Four (Week 5)
Growing My Wealth With Liberty

Read this out loud when you arise; from "I promise to" through "I always keep my promises". Be certain to sign it and include your name in the reading out loud.

I promise to follow these 3 steps today
1. I read the Fifth Verity two times today, first thing in the morning and aloud in the evening just before I go to bed.
2. I read my "Intention" card three times today with enthusiasm
3. As I go through my day, I identify liberty with magnifying glass focus all day

_____

I always keep my promises

Here are a few examples of acts of liberty. Children being themselves, people who make their requests clear, pets, non-self conscious behavior, people making fun of themselves, confidence, people taking risks, encouragement, all animals... Note each one and check off a box for each example you find during the day. Find some of your own! The more you identify liberty the more liberty you will experience. Look for it everywhere and use the immutable Law of Growth to grow it within your heart.

OOOOO OOOOO OOOOO OOOOO OOOOO

Before your nighttime read and sitting still, check off the examples you saw. Each day the number you spot will grow if you focus.
Jot down the best example you observed today of liberty.

Day Five (Week 5)
Growing My Wealth With Liberty

Read this out loud when you arise; from "I promise to" through "I always keep my promises". Be certain to sign it and include your name in the reading out loud.

I promise to follow these 3 steps today

1. I read the Fifth Verity two times today, first thing in the morning and aloud in the evening just before I go to bed.
2. I read my "Intention" card three times today with enthusiasm
3. As I go through my day, I identify liberty with magnifying glass focus all day

_____

I always keep my promises

Here are a few of examples of acts of liberty. Children being themselves, people who make their requests clear, pets, non-self conscious behavior, people making fun of themselves, confidence, people taking risks, encouragement, all animals... Note each one and check off a box for each example you find during the day. Find some of your own! The more you identify liberty the more liberty you will experience. Look for it everywhere and use the immutable Law of Growth to grow it within your heart

OOOOO OOOOO OOOOO OOOOO OOOOO

Before your nighttime read and sitting still, check off the examples you saw. Each day the number you spot will grow if you focus.
Jot down the best example you observed today of liberty.

135

Day Six (Week 5)
Growing My Wealth With Liberty

Read this out loud when you arise; from "I promise to" through "I always keep my promises". Be certain to sign it and include your name in the reading out loud.

I promise to follow these 3 steps today

1. I read the Fifth Verity two times today, first thing in the morning and aloud in the evening just before I go to bed.
2. I read my "Intention" card three times today with enthusiasm
3. As I go through my day, I identify liberty with magnifying glass focus all day

_____

I always keep my promises

Here are a few examples of acts of liberty. Children being themselves, people who make their requests clear, pets, non-self conscious behavior, people making fun of themselves, confidence, people taking risks, encouragement, all animals... Note each one and check off a box for each example you find during the day. Find some of your own! The more you identify liberty the more liberty you will experience. Look for it everywhere and use the immutable Law of Growth to grow it within your heart.

OOOOO OOOOO OOOOO OOOOO OOOOO

Before your nighttime read and sitting still, check off the examples you saw. Each day the number you spot will grow if you focus.
Jot down the best example you observed today of liberty.

Day Seven (Week 5)
Growing My Wealth With Liberty

Read this out loud when you arise; from "I promise to" through "I always keep my promises". Be certain to sign it and include your name in the reading out loud.

I promise to follow these 3 steps today
1. I read the Fifth Verity two times today, first thing in the morning and aloud in the evening just before I go to bed.
2. I read my "Intention" card three times today with enthusiasm
3. As I go through my day, I identify liberty with magnifying glass focus all day

_____

I always keep my promises

Here are a few of examples of acts of liberty. Children being themselves, people who make their requests clear, pets, non-self conscious behavior, people making fun of themselves, confidence, people taking risks, encouragement, all animals... Note each one and check off a box for each example you find during the day. Find some of your own! The more you identify liberty the more liberty you will experience. Look for it everywhere and use the immutable Law of Growth to grow it within your heart

O O O O O   O O O O O   O O O O O   O O O O O   O O O O O

Before your nighttime read and sitting still, check off the examples you saw. Each day the number you spot will grow if you focus.
Jot down the best example you observed today of liberty.

137

The Sixth of the 13 Riches
The Labor of Love

There is an old saying, "faith will move mountains but you need to bring a shovel." While holding your intention is crucial and directing your faith constantly towards the desired outcome is essential, it is action that manifests your objective. We must supply the energy to the tasks before us as they reveal themselves.

You have already conditioned yourself to take action without hesitation with the Fourth Verity but the real riches in achieving your intention are found in loving the labor and loving the motive you hold for your intention. Greater than the feelings you experience for the achievement of materializing your intention is the journey to that destination. The truly wealthy view each step, each task as a labor of love. Experiencing joy in meeting challenges, learning lessons from mistakes, seeing setbacks as refining the steps to victory and running to obstacles with excitement is the profile of the wealthy; they see all these things as a labor of love.

They love the reason they are doing what must be done. They own and love their real reason for the hope of achievement. They love how attaining their intention will affect their loved ones. And this labor of love is true passion. They draw immense satisfaction from completing their work for the day because they do the best they are capable of doing, giving themselves fully to each task with joy.

There once was an important politician who was walking through the workers that were building a massive structure that would take two or more generations of workers to complete. They were cutting massive blocks of granite on a very hot, humid day. The politician saw the strain and sweat and pain in the workers faces. He asked one man, "What are you doing?" The man replied, "Cutting stone." He asked another the same question and the man replied, "Cutting stone." He asked over 10 men the same question and got the same response. He then saw another man, cutting stone, and working harder than all the workers. This man was smiling and humming. "What are you doing?" The man replied with a big smile, "I'm building a cathedral!"

Day One (Week 6)
Growing My Wealth A Labor of Love

Read this out loud when you arise; from "I promise to" through "I always keep my promises". Be certain to sign it and include your name in the reading out loud.

I promise to follow these 3 steps today

1. I read the Sixth Verity two times today, first thing in the morning and aloud in the evening just before I go to bed.
2. I read my "Intention" card three times today with enthusiasm
3. As I go through my day, I identify labors of love both in work and home

_____

I always keep my promises

Here are a few examples of labors of love. A mother caring for her children, a cheerful worker, people good at their job, workers who smile, coaches, artists, musicians, athletes, merchants who love what they offer... Note each one and check off a box for each example you find during the day. Find some of your own! The more you identify passion for the labor, the more love you will have for your work. If your work becomes a pleasure to perform you will run to challenges rather than away from them and manifest intention faster. Let your passion move beyond the intention and you will acquire a special wealth that lifts your spirits daily and provides infinite energy.

○○○○○ ○○○○○ ○○○○○ ○○○○○ ○○○○○

Before your nighttime read and sitting still, check off the examples you saw. Each day the number you spot will grow if you focus.
Jot down the best example you observed today of a labor of love.

140

Day Two (Week 6)
Growing My Wealth A Labor of Love

Read this out loud when you arise; from "I promise to" through "I always keep my promises". Be certain to sign it and include your name in the reading out loud.

I promise to follow these 3 steps today

1. I read the Sixth Verity two times today, first thing in the morning and aloud in the evening just before I go to bed.
2. I read my "Intention" card three times today with enthusiasm
3. As I go through my day, I identify labors of love both in work and home

_____

I always keep my promises

Here are a few examples of labors of love. A mother caring for her children, a cheerful worker, people good at their job, workers who smile, coaches, artists, musicians, athletes, merchants who love what they offer... Note each one and check off a box for each example you find during the day. Find some of your own! The more you identify passion for the labor, the more love you will have for your work. If your work becomes a pleasure to perform you will run to challenges rather than away from them and manifest intention faster. Let your passion move beyond the intention and you will acquire a special wealth that lifts your spirits daily and provides infinite energy.

○○○○○ ○○○○○ ○○○○○ ○○○○○ ○○○○○

Before your nighttime read and sitting still, check off the examples you saw. Each day the number you spot will grow if you focus.
Jot down the best example you observed today of a labor of love.

Day Three (Week 6)
Growing My Wealth A Labor of Love

Read this out loud when you arise; from "I promise to" through "I always keep my promises". Be certain to sign it and include your name in the reading out loud.

I promise to follow these 3 steps today

1. I read the Sixth Verity two times today, first thing in the morning and aloud in the evening just before I go to bed.
2. I read my "Intention" card three times today with enthusiasm
3. As I go through my day, I identify labors of love both in work and home

———————————————

I always keep my promises

Here are a few examples of labors of love. A mother caring for her children, a cheerful worker, people good at their job, workers who smile, coaches, artists, musicians, athletes, merchants who love what they offer... Note each one and check off a box for each example you find during the day. Find some of your own! The more you identify passion for the labor, the more love you will have for your work. If your work becomes a pleasure to perform you will run to challenges rather than away from them and manifest intention faster. Let your passion move beyond the intention and you will acquire a special wealth that lifts your spirits daily and provides infinite energy.

OOOOO OOOOO OOOOO OOOOO OOOOO

Before your nighttime read and sitting still, check off the examples you saw. Each day the number you spot will grow if you focus.
Jot down the best example you observed today of a labor of love.

142

Day Four (Week 6)
Growing My Wealth A Labor of Love

Read this out loud when you arise; from "I promise to" through "I always keep my promises". Be certain to sign it and include your name in the reading out loud.

I promise to follow these 3 steps today

1. I read the Sixth Verity two times today, first thing in the morning and aloud in the evening just before I go to bed.
2. I read my "Intention" card three times today with enthusiasm
3. As I go through my day, I identify labors of love both in work and home

_____

I always keep my promises

Here are a few examples of labors of love. A mother caring for her children, a cheerful worker, people good at their job, workers who smile, coaches, artists, musicians, athletes, merchants who love what they offer... Note each one and check off a box for each example you find during the day. Find some of your own! The more you identify passion for the labor, the more love you will have for your work. If your work becomes a pleasure to perform you will run to challenges rather than away from them and manifest intention faster. Let your passion move beyond the intention and you will acquire a special wealth that lifts your spirits daily and provides infinite energy.

OOOOO OOOOO OOOOO OOOOO OOOOO

Before your nighttime read and sitting still, check off the examples you saw. Each day the number you spot will grow if you focus.

Jot down the best example you observed today of a labor of love.

143

Day Five (Week 6)
Growing My Wealth A Labor of Love

Read this out loud when you arise; from "I promise to" through "I always keep my promises". Be certain to sign it and include your name in the reading out loud.

I promise to follow these 3 steps today

1. *I read the Sixth Verity two times today, first thing in the morning and aloud in the evening just before I go to bed.*
2. *I read my "Intention" card three times today with enthusiasm*
3. *As I go through my day, I identify labors of love both in work and home*

_____

I always keep my promises

Here are a few examples of labors of love. A mother caring for her children, a cheerful worker, people good at their job, workers who smile, coaches, artists, musicians, athletes, merchants who love what they offer... Note each one and check off a box for each example you find during the day. Find some of your own! The more you identify passion for the labor, the more love you will have for your work. If your work becomes a pleasure to perform you will run to challenges rather than away from them and manifest intention faster. Let your passion move beyond the intention and you will acquire a special wealth that lifts your spirits daily and provides infinite energy.

○○○○○　○○○○○　○○○○○　○○○○○　○○○○○

Before your nighttime read and sitting still, check off the examples you saw. Each day the number you spot will grow if you focus.

Jot down the best example you observed today of a labor of love.

Day Six (Week 6)
Growing My Wealth A Labor of Love

Read this out loud when you arise; from "I promise to" through "I always keep my promises". Be certain to sign it and include your name in the reading out loud.

I promise to follow these 3 steps today

1. I read the Sixth Verity two times today, first thing in the morning and aloud in the evening just before I go to bed.
2. I read my "Intention" card three times today with enthusiasm
3. As I go through my day, I identify labors of love both in work and home

_____

I always keep my promises

Here are a few examples of labors of love. A mother caring for her children, a cheerful worker, people good at their job, workers who smile, coaches, artists, musicians, athletes, merchants who love what they offer... Note each one and check off a box for each example you find during the day. Find some of your own! The more you identify passion for the labor, the more love you will have for your work. If your work becomes a pleasure to perform you will run to challenges rather than away from them and manifest intention faster. Let your passion move beyond the intention and you will acquire a special wealth that lifts your spirits daily and provides infinite energy.

○○○○○ ○○○○○ ○○○○○ ○○○○○ ○○○○○

Before your nighttime read and sitting still, check off the examples you saw. Each day the number you spot will grow if you focus.

Jot down the best example you observed today of a labor of love.

Day Seven (Week 6)
Growing My Wealth A Labor of Love

Read this out loud when you arise; from "I promise to" through "I always keep my promises". Be certain to sign it and include your name in the reading out loud.

I promise to follow these 3 steps today

1. *I read the Sixth Verity two times today, first thing in the morning and aloud in the evening just before I go to bed.*
2. *I read my "Intention" card three times today with enthusiasm*
3. *As I go through my day, I identify labors of love both in work and home*

_____

I always keep my promises

Here are a few examples of labors of love. A mother caring for her children, a cheerful worker, people good at their job, workers who smile, coaches, artists, musicians, athletes, merchants who love what they offer... Note each one and check off a box for each example you find during the day. Find some of your own! The more you identify passion for the labor, the more love you will have for your work. If your work becomes a pleasure to perform you will run to challenges rather than away from them and manifest intention faster. Let your passion move beyond the intention and you will acquire a special wealth that lifts your spirits daily and provides infinite energy.

○○○○○ ○○○○○ ○○○○○ ○○○○○ ○○○○○

Before your nighttime read and sitting still, check off the examples you saw. Each day the number you spot will grow if you focus.

Jot down the best example you observed today of a labor of love.

The Seventh of the 13 Riches
Sound Harmony In All Relationships

Can one have any greater wealth than the wealth that is yielded by friendship? And is there anything more rewarding than the intimate relationship with a mate? Can anything match the richness of meaningful relationships with our children?

To have a wealth of these significant relationships that enrich us beyond measure we must become a great friend. To be a great friend we demonstrate harmony in all relationships. The truly wealthy love all and respect all people. Being in harmony with a loved one on a wonderful day is not the measure of our ability be to a great friend. To render unconditional love when challenges arise is the true indicator of our willingness to be a great friend.

And of people who see things very differently? We must accept and celebrate those differences, bring peace and harmony with our heart when our head wants to attack, belittle or judge. Acceptance is the handmaiden to harmony. Those who transform The Map into wealth know that if they accept everyone, give the gift of love in their minds towards all people, that their ability to be a great friend rises tenfold. By improving ourselves, all things improve. Your good relationships become better and your better relationships become great. And you become overwhelmed with gratitude for the richly textured blessings the people in your life pour over you, a harmonious friend.

How have the great ones of great wealth done it? They judge no one and see The Source of All Good in everyone. The key to the treasure chest of harmony in all relationships is replacing judgment with love. When we celebrate the differences by bringing harmony to all we meet, others feel safe, respected and treasured.

Day One (Week 7)
Growing My Wealth With Harmony In All Relationships

Read this out loud when you arise; from "I promise to" through "I always keep my promises". Be certain to sign it and include your name in the reading out loud.

I promise to follow these 3 steps today

1. I read the Seventh Verity two times today, first thing in the morning and aloud in the evening just before I go to bed.
2. I read my "Intention" card three times today with enthusiasm.
3. As I go through my day, I identify harmony in relationships.

_____

I always keep my promises

Here are a few examples of harmony. People shaking hands, hugging, people listening, making eye contact, helping one another, laughing together, teams, people saying yes, nature... Note each one and check off a box for each example you find during the day. Find some of your own! The more you identify harmony the more harmony will permeate your life. Judge no one. Let your harmony infect others and notice how quickly focusing on harmony pays rich dividends for mastering the Law of Growth with magnifying glass focus.

OOOOO OOOOO OOOOO OOOOO OOOOO

Before your nighttime read and sitting still, check off the examples you saw. Each day the number you spot will grow if you focus.
Jot down the best example you observed today of harmony.

Day Two (Week 7)
Growing My Wealth With Harmony In All Relationships

Read this out loud when you arise; from "I promise to" through "I always keep my promises". Be certain to sign it and include your name in the reading out loud.

I promise to follow these 3 steps today

1. *I read the Seventh Verity two times today, first thing in the morning and aloud in the evening just before I go to bed.*
2. *I read my "Intention" card three times today with enthusiasm.*
3. *As I go through my day, I identify harmony in relationships.*

_____

I always keep my promises

Here are a few examples of harmony. People shaking hands, hugging, people listening, making eye contact, helping one another, laughing together, teams, people saying yes, nature... Note each one and check off a box for each example you find during the day. Find some of your own! The more you identify harmony the more harmony will permeate your life. Judge no one. Let your harmony infect others and notice how quickly focusing on harmony pays rich dividends for mastering the Law of Growth with magnifying glass focus.

○○○○○　○○○○○　○○○○○　○○○○○　○○○○○

Before your nighttime read and sitting still, check off the examples you saw. Each day the number you spot will grow if you focus.
Jot down the best example you observed today of harmony.

Day Three (Week 7)
Growing My Wealth With Harmony In All Relationships

Read this out loud when you arise; from "I promise to" through "I always keep my promises". Be certain to sign it and include your name in the reading out loud.

I promise to follow these 3 steps today

1. *I read the Seventh Verity two times today, first thing in the morning and aloud in the evening just before I go to bed.*
2. *I read my "Intention" card three times today with enthusiasm.*
3. *As I go through my day, I identify harmony in relationships.*

_____

I always keep my promises

Here are a few examples of harmony. People shaking hands, hugging, people listening, making eye contact, helping one another, laughing together, teams, people saying yes, nature... Note each one and check off a box for each example you find during the day. Find some of your own! The more you identify harmony the more harmony will permeate your life. Judge no one. Let your harmony infect others and notice how quickly focusing on harmony pays rich dividends for mastering the Law of Growth with magnifying glass focus.

○○○○○ ○○○○○ ○○○○○ ○○○○○ ○○○○○

Before your nighttime read and sitting still, check off the examples you saw. Each day the number you spot will grow if you focus.
Jot down the best example you observed today of harmony.

150

Day Four (Week 7)
Growing My Wealth With Harmony In All Relationships

Read this out loud when you arise; from "I promise to" through "I always keep my promises". Be certain to sign it and include your name in the reading out loud.

I promise to follow these 3 steps today

1. I read the Seventh Verity two times today, first thing in the morning and aloud in the evening just before I go to bed.
2. I read my "Intention" card three times today with enthusiasm.
3. As I go through my day, I identify harmony in relationships.

_____

I always keep my promises

Here are a few examples of harmony. People shaking hands, hugging, people listening, making eye contact, helping one another, laughing together, teams, people saying yes, nature... Note each one and check off a box for each example you find during the day. Find some of your own! The more you identify harmony the more harmony will permeate your life. Judge no one. Let your harmony infect others and notice how quickly focusing on harmony pays rich dividends for mastering the Law of Growth with magnifying glass focus.

○○○○○　○○○○○　○○○○○　○○○○○　○○○○○

Before your nighttime read and sitting still, check off the examples you saw. Each day the number you spot will grow if you focus.
Jot down the best example you observed today of harmony.

151

Day Five (Week 7)
Growing My Wealth With Harmony In All Relationships

Read this out loud when you arise; from "I promise to" through "I always keep my promises". Be certain to sign it and include your name in the reading out loud.

I promise to follow these 3 steps today

1. I read the Seventh Verity two times today, first thing in the morning and aloud in the evening just before I go to bed.
2. I read my "Intention" card three times today with enthusiasm.
3. As I go through my day, I identify harmony in relationships.

_____

I always keep my promises

Here are a few examples of harmony. People shaking hands, hugging, people listening, making eye contact, helping one another, laughing together, teams, people saying yes, nature... Note each one and check off a box for each example you find during the day. Find some of your own! The more you identify harmony the more harmony will permeate your life. Judge no one. Let your harmony infect others and notice how quickly focusing on harmony pays rich dividends for mastering the Law of Growth with magnifying glass focus.

○○○○○　○○○○○　○○○○○　○○○○○　○○○○○

Before your nighttime read and sitting still, check off the examples you saw. Each day the number you spot will grow if you focus.
Jot down the best example you observed today of harmony.

Day Six (Week 7)
Growing My Wealth With Harmony In All Relationships

Read this out loud when you arise; from "I promise to" through "I always keep my promises". Be certain to sign it and include your name in the reading out loud.

I promise to follow these 3 steps today

1. I read the Seventh Verity two times today, first thing in the morning and aloud in the evening just before I go to bed.
2. I read my "Intention" card three times today with enthusiasm.
3. As I go through my day, I identify harmony in relationships.

_____

I always keep my promises

Here are a few examples of harmony. People shaking hands, hugging, people listening, making eye contact, helping one another, laughing together, teams, people saying yes, nature... Note each one and check off a box for each example you find during the day. Find some of your own! The more you identify harmony the more harmony will permeate your life. Judge no one. Let your harmony infect others and notice how quickly focusing on harmony pays rich dividends for mastering the Law of Growth with magnifying glass focus.

○○○○○ ○○○○○ ○○○○○ ○○○○○ ○○○○○

Before your nighttime read and sitting still, check off the examples you saw. Each day the number you spot will grow if you focus.

Jot down the best example you observed today of harmony.

Day Seven (Week 7)
Growing My Wealth With Harmony In All Relationships

Read this out loud when you arise; from "I promise to" through "I always keep my promises". Be certain to sign it and include your name in the reading out loud.

I promise to follow these 3 steps today

1. I read the Seventh Verity two times today, first thing in the morning and aloud in the evening just before I go to bed.
2. I read my "Intention" card three times today with enthusiasm.
3. As I go through my day, I identify harmony in relationships.

_____

I always keep my promises

Here are a few examples of harmony. People shaking hands, hugging, people listening, making eye contact, helping one another, laughing together, teams, people saying yes, nature... Note each one and check off a box for each example you find during the day. Find some of your own! The more you identify harmony the more harmony will permeate your life. Judge no one. Let your harmony infect others and notice how quickly focusing on harmony pays rich dividends for mastering the Law of Growth with magnifying glass focus.

○○○○○ ○○○○○ ○○○○○ ○○○○○ ○○○○○

Before your nighttime read and sitting still, check off the examples you saw. Each day the number you spot will grow if you focus.

Jot down the best example you observed today of harmony.

The Eight of the 13 Riches
Growing My Wealth With Self Disciplin

The most pivotal behavior in unilateral success is self-discipline. With our health, with our business and with our relationships, self-discipline reigns as the foremost factor in determining success or failure.

You have already begun to establish this with the Fifth Verity, First Things First. Is it a list or is it a habit? It all depends on you exerting your will, your self-discipline, not the list. Will you take care of the tasks as if you are the person you intend to become or will you opt for distractions and make foolish promises to double your efforts tomorrow? The world is full of temptations and self-discipline is the only way to maintain that magnifying glass focus on the tasks that will manifest your intention and grow your wealth.

Temptation is excellent at its job. Your path to the 13 Riches and your intention is a straight, downhill run. Temptation cannot get on your path; you must get off your path to succumb to temptation. Let's again acknowledge that temptation is good at its job, very good. So how do we avoid it and stay on the path to intention and wealth? Self-discipline!

To develop the riches of self-discipline the great ones discovered that the root factor was developing the skill of delaying gratification. It may be tempting to overeat, play before work is done, skip our exercise routine... tempting to do the more comfortable, easier things rather than the task in front of us because it feels like we will get instant gratification from it. The wealthy ones pause, picture their intention in the face of instant gratification, inhale slowly and realize in that moment that they have a choice. They can surrender to temptation and take the instant gratification or they can delay gratification. By picturing and imagining how they will feel when they obtain wealth and when they achieve their intention, they make the correct choice; they delay their gratification for the greater satisfaction of achievement, wealth and peace of mind. The skill of delaying gratification is the fountainhead of the riches of self-discipline.

Day One (Week 8)
Growing My Wealth With Self-discipline

Read this out loud when you arise; from "I promise to" through "I always keep my promises". Be certain to sign it and include your name in the reading out loud.

I promise to follow these 3 steps today

1.   I read the First Verity two times today, first thing in the morning and aloud in the evening just before I go to bed.

2.   I read my "Intention" card three times today with enthusiasm

3.   As I go through my day, I identify self-discipline

_____

I always keep my promises

Here are a few examples of self-discipline and its root, delaying gratification: exercises, eating in moderation, doing one thing at a time, complete and undivided attention, declining desserts, declining invitations to be social until work is complete, patience, people who are well prepared. Note each one and check off a box for each example you find during the day. Find some of your own! The more examples of self-discipline you identify, the faster and stronger it will grow in you.

OOOOO OOOOO OOOOO OOOOO OOOOO

Before your nighttime read and sitting still, check off the examples you saw. Each day the number you spot will grow if you focus.

Jot down the best example you observed today of delaying gratification.

Day Two (Week 8)
Growing My Wealth With Self-discipline

Read this out loud when you arise; from "I promise to" through "I always keep my promises". Be certain to sign it and include your name in the reading out loud.

I promise to follow these 3 steps today

1. I read the Second Verity two times today, first thing in the morning and aloud in the evening just before I go to bed.

2. I read my "Intention" card three times today with enthusiasm

3. As I go through my day, I identify self-discipline

_____

I always keep my promises

Here are a few examples of self-discipline and its root, delaying gratification... exercises, eating in moderation, doing one thing at a time, complete and undivided attention, declining desserts, declining invitations to be social until work is complete, patience, people who are well prepared. Note each one and check off a box for each example you find during the day. Find some of your own! The more you identify self-discipline the faster and strong it will grow in you.

○○○○○   ○○○○○   ○○○○○   ○○○○○   ○○○○○

Before your nighttime read and sitting still, check off the examples you saw. Each day the number you spot will grow if you focus.

Jot down the best example you observed today of delaying gratification.

Day Three (Week 8)
Growing My Wealth With Self-discipline

Read this out loud when you arise; from "I promise to" through "I always keep my promises". Be certain to sign it and include your name in the reading out loud.

I promise to follow these 3 steps today

1. I read the Third Verity two times today, first thing in the morning and aloud in the evening just before I go to bed.

2. I read my "Intention" card three times today with enthusiasm.

3. As I go through my day, I identify self-discipline.

_____

I always keep my promises

Here are a couple of examples of self-discipline and its root, delaying gratification... exercises, eating in moderation, doing one thing at a time, complete and undivided attention, declining desserts, declining invitations to be social until work is complete, patience, people who are well prepared. Note each one and check off a box for each example you find during the day. Find some of your own! The more you identify self-discipline the faster and strong it will grow in you.

OOOOO   OOOOO   OOOOO   OOOOO   OOOOO

Before your nighttime read and sitting still, check off the examples you saw. Each day the number you spot will grow if you focus.
Jot down the best example you observed today of delaying gratification.

Day Four (Week 8)
Growing My Wealth With Self-discipline

Read this out loud when you arise; from "I promise to" through "I always keep my promises". Be certain to sign it and include your name in the reading out loud.

I promise to follow these 3 steps today

1. I read the Fourth Verity two times today, first thing in the morning and aloud in the evening just before I go to bed.

2. I read my "Intention" card three times today with enthusiasm

3. As I go through my day, I identify self-discipline.

_____

I always keep my promises

Here are few of examples of self-discipline and its root, delaying gratification... exercises, eating in moderation, doing one thing at a time, complete and undivided attention, declining desserts, declining invitations to be social until work is complete, patience, people who are well prepared. Note each one and check off a box for each example you find during the day. Find some of your own! The more you identify self-discipline the faster and strong it will grow in you.

O O O O O   O O O O O   O O O O O   O O O O O   O O O O O

Before your nighttime read and sitting still, check off the examples you saw. Each day the number you spot will grow if you focus.
Jot down the best example you observed today of delaying gratification.

Day Five (Week 8)
Growing My Wealth With Self-discipline

Read this out loud when you arise; from "I promise to" through "I always keep my promises". Be certain to sign it and include your name in the reading out loud.

I promise to follow these 3 steps today

1. I read the Fifth Verity two times today, first thing in the morning and aloud in the evening just before I go to bed.

2. I read my "Intention" card three times today with enthusiasm

3. As I go through my day, I identify self-discipline

_____

I always keep my promises

Here are a few examples of self-discipline and its root, delaying gratification... exercises, eating in moderation, doing one thing at a time, complete and undivided attention, declining desserts, declining invitations to be social until work is complete, patience, people who are well prepared. Note each one and check off a box for each example you find during the day. Find some of your own! The more you identify self-discipline the faster and strong it will grow in you.

○○○○○   ○○○○○   ○○○○○   ○○○○○   ○○○○○

Before your nighttime read and sitting still, check off the examples you saw. Each day the number you spot will grow if you focus.

Jot down the best example you observed today of delaying gratification.

Day Six (Week 8)
Growing My Wealth With Self-discipline

Read this out loud when you arise; from "I promise to" through "I always keep my promises". Be certain to sign it and include your name in the reading out loud.

I promise to follow these 3 steps today

1. I read the Sixth Verity two times today, first thing in the morning and aloud in the evening just before I go to bed.

2. I read my "Intention" card three times today with enthusiasm

3. As I go through my day, I identify self-discipline

_____

I always keep my promises

Here are a few examples of self-discipline and its root, delaying gratification... exercises, eating in moderation, doing one thing at a time, complete and undivided attention, declining desserts, declining invitations to be social until work is complete, patience, people who are well prepared...note each one and check off a box for each example you find during the day. Find some of your own! The more you identify self-discipline the faster and strong it will grow in you.

○○○○○ ○○○○○ ○○○○○ ○○○○○ ○○○○○

Before your nighttime read and sitting still, check off the examples you saw. Each day the number you spot will grow if you focus.

Jot down the best example you observed today of delaying gratification.

Day Seven (Week 8)
Growing My Wealth With Self-discipline

Read this out loud when you arise; from "I promise to" through "I always keep my promises". Be certain to sign it and include your name in the reading out loud.

I promise to follow these 3 steps today

1. I read the Seventh Verity two times today, first thing in the morning and aloud in the evening just before I go to bed.

2. I read my "Intention" card three times today with enthusiasm

3. As I go through my day, I identify self-discipline

_____

I always keep my promises

Here are a few examples of self-discipline and its root, delaying gratification... exercises, eating in moderation, doing one thing at a time, complete and undivided attention, declining desserts, declining invitations to be social until work is complete, patience, people who are well prepared. Note each one and check off a box for each example you find during the day. Find some of your own! The more you identify self-discipline the faster and strong it will grow in you.

○○○○○ ○○○○○ ○○○○○ ○○○○○ ○○○○○

Before your nighttime read and sitting still, check off the examples you saw. Each day the number you spot will grow if you focus.

Jot down the best example you observed today of delaying gratification.

163

The Ninth of the 13 Riches
Growing My Wealth With Kindness

The overall perception we have of the world creates a massive part of the environment within our mind. As you know from Verity Four, what belongs in an environment shows up and flourishes, what does not belong in an environment must perish. We all have a choice to make about the world and that choice sets the general environment in our world within. If we believe the world is perfect, yet incomplete then building towards our worthwhile intention, harmonious with The Source, becomes automatic... it belongs there. If, on the other hand, we believe the world is decaying, going to hell and evil, growing something wonderful in our world within is simply not possible.

The great navigators of The Map realize these things and take it upon themselves to help complete the perfect world The Source has provided. They make the world a better place by making the world within their minds a better place. The riches of kindness help all of us believe the world is good, evolving and getting better. With this belief, our world within grows great things effortlessly. How do the great ones do it?

They understand kindness is the universal language, draws the best out of people and helps complete and perfect the world. Kindness is language that even the deaf can hear, a language even the blind can see. What is remembered above achievement, position and influence is their kindness. Your kindness will be your legacy, make it remarkable by forgetting self and thinking of others. It will return to you ten-fold and as it does, it will train your world within that the world truly is perfect and all it will take to complete its perfection are random acts of kindness delivered in copious quantities. Take joy in doing yours everyday.

Day One (Week 9)
Growing My Wealth With Kindness

Read this out loud when you arise; from "I promise to" through "I always keep my promises". Be certain to sign it and include your name in the reading out loud.

I promise to follow these 4 steps today

1. I read the First Verity two times today, first thing in the morning and aloud in the evening just before I go to bed.

2. I read my "Intention" card three times today with enthusiasm

3. I commit to doing two or more random acts of kindness everyday

4. As I go through my day, I identify kindness everywhere

_____

I always keep my promises

Here are a few examples of kindness. Manners, generosity, affection, hospitality, care, charity. Note each one and check off a box for each example you find during the day. Find some of your own! The more examples of kindness you identify, the kinder becomes the world and you realize how everything that is good is also incredibly abundant.

○○○○○ ○○○○○ ○○○○○ ○○○○○ ○○○○○

Before your nighttime read and sitting still, check off the examples you saw. Each day the number you spot will grow if you focus.
Jot down the best example you observed today of kindness.

Day Two (Week 9)
Growing My Wealth With Kindness

Read this out loud when you arise; from "I promise to" through "I always keep my promises". Be certain to sign it and include your name in the reading out loud.

I promise to follow these 4 steps today

1. I read the Second Verity two times today, first thing in the morning and aloud in the evening just before I go to bed.

2. I read my "Intention" card three times today with enthusiasm

3. I commit two or more random acts of kindness everyday

4. As I go through my day, I identify kindness everywhere

_____

I always keep my promises

Here are a few examples of kindness. Manners, generosity, affection, hospitality, care, charity. Note each one and check off a box for each example you find during the day. Find some of your own! The more you identify kindness the more kind the world becomes and you will realize how everything that is good is also incredibly abundant.

○○○○○ ○○○○○ ○○○○○ ○○○○○ ○○○○○

Before your nighttime read and sitting still, check off the examples you saw. Each day the number you spot will grow if you focus.
Jot down the best example you observed today of kindness.

Day Three (Week 9)
Growing My Wealth With Kindness

Read this out loud when you arise; from "I promise to" through "I always keep my promises". Be certain to sign it and include your name in the reading out loud.

I promise to follow these 4 steps today

1. I read the Third Verity two times today, first thing in the morning and aloud in the evening just before I go to bed.

2. I read my "Intention" card three times today with enthusiasm

3. I commit two or more random acts of kindness everyday

4. As I go through my day, I identify kindness everywhere

_____

I always keep my promises

Here are a few examples of kindness. Manners, generosity, affection, hospitality, care, charity. Note each one and check off a box for each example you find during the day. Find some of your own! The more you identify kindness the more kind the world becomes and you will realize how everything that is good is also incredibly abundant.

OOOOO OOOOO OOOOO OOOOO OOOOO

Before your nighttime read and sitting still, check off the examples you saw. Each day the number you spot will grow if you focus.

Jot down the best example you observed today of kindness.

Day Four (Week 9)
Growing My Wealth With Kindness

Read this out loud when you arise; from "I promise to" through "I always keep my promises". Be certain to sign it and include your name in the reading out loud.

I promise to follow these 4 steps today

1. I read the Fourth Verity two times today, first thing in the morning and aloud in the evening just before I go to bed.

2. I read my "Intention" card three times today with enthusiasm

3. I commit two or more random acts of kindness everyday

4. As I go through my day, I identify kindness everywhere

_____

I always keep my promises

Here are a few examples of kindness. Manners, generosity, affection, hospitality, care, charity. Note each one and check off a box for each example you find during the day. Find some of your own! The more you identify kindness the more kind the world becomes and you will realize how everything that is good is also incredibly abundant.

○○○○○ ○○○○○ ○○○○○ ○○○○○ ○○○○○

Before your nighttime read and sitting still, check off the examples you saw. Each day the number you spot will grow if you focus.
Jot down the best example you observed today of kindness.

Day Five (Week 9)
Growing My Wealth With Kindness

Read this out loud when you arise; from "I promise to" through "I always keep my promises". Be certain to sign it and include your name in the reading out loud.

I promise to follow these 4 steps today

1. I read the Fifth Verity two times today, first thing in the morning and aloud in the evening just before I go to bed.

2. I read my "Intention" card three times today with enthusiasm

3. I commit two or more random acts of kindness everyday

4. As I go through my day, I identify kindness everywhere

_____

I always keep my promises

Here are a few examples of kindness. Manners, generosity, affection, hospitality, care, charity. Note each one and check off a box for each example you find during the day. Find some of your own! The more you identify kindness the more kind the world becomes and you will realize how everything that is good is also incredibly abundant.

○ ○ ○ ○ ○   ○ ○ ○ ○ ○   ○ ○ ○ ○ ○   ○ ○ ○ ○ ○   ○ ○ ○ ○ ○

Before your nighttime read and sitting still, check off the examples you saw. Each day the number you spot will grow if you focus.
Jot down the best example you observed today of kindness.

169

Day Six (Week 9)
Growing My Wealth With Kindness

Read this out loud when you arise; from "I promise to" through "I always keep my promises". Be certain to sign it and include your name in the reading out loud.

I promise to follow these 4 steps today

1. I read the Sixth Verity two times today, first thing in the morning and aloud in the evening just before I go to bed.

2. I read my "Intention" card three times today with enthusiasm

3. I commit two or more random acts of kindness everyday

4. As I go through my day, I identify kindness everywhere

_____

I always keep my promises

Here are a few examples of kindness. Manners, generosity, affection, hospitality, care, charity. Note each one and check off a box for each example you find during the day. Find some of your own! The more you identify kindness the more kind the world becomes and you will realize how everything that is good is also incredibly abundant.

○○○○○ ○○○○○ ○○○○○ ○○○○○ ○○○○○

Before your nighttime read and sitting still, check off the examples you saw. Each day the number you spot will grow if you focus.
Jot down the best example you observed today of kindness.

Day Seven (Week 9)
Growing My Wealth With Kindness

Read this out loud when you arise; from "I promise to" through "I always keep my promises". Be certain to sign it and include your name in the reading out loud.

I promise to follow these 4 steps today

1. I read the Seventh Verity two times today, first thing in the morning and aloud in the evening just before I go to bed.

2. I read my "Intention" card three times today with enthusiasm

3. I commit two or more random acts of kindness everyday

4. As I go through my day, I identify kindness everywhere

_____

I always keep my promises

Here are a couple of examples of kindness. Manners, generosity, affection, hospitality, care, charity. Note each one and check off a box for each example you find during the day. Find some of your own! The more you identify kindness the more kind the world becomes and you will realize how everything that is good is also incredibly abundant.

OOOOO OOOOO OOOOO OOOOO OOOOO

Before your nighttime read and sitting still, check off the examples you saw. Each day the number you spot will grow if you focus.

Jot down the best example you observed today of kindness.

The Secont of the 13 Riches
Hope

Those who accumulated wealth beyond measure know the deeper meaning of hope. There are times in all people's lives, such as the loss of a loved one, failure in business, inability to meet financial obligations when the only thing that keeps one going is that there is hope... we hope there is hope. The hope of achievement, the hope of a loving relationship, the hope of change in a challenging situation are all wonderful evidences of the human spirit. And while wonderful, hope at these moments is rarely realized until we find the deeper wisdom within hope.

So what is this deeper meaning of hope that the great achievers understood? They know that each letter in the word "hope" represents a clear direction for those who have decided to claim the 13 Riches of Life.

H – Help O – Other P – People E – Evolve

To experience the riches of hope, means helping other people evolve with encouraging words, hands on help and by sharing one's experience, strength and actualized hope.

Hearts get broken, jobs get lost and people fail but you already know that things turn out for the best for those who make the best of the way things turn out. Often a kind word during a trying time or during the pursuit of a dream is great. It encourages willingness to press on. Yet real hope is being willing to Help Other People Evolve by sharing your wisdom, lending a helping hand or working with them towards the things they are hoping for. And, as the night follows the day, the more HOPE you give, the more it will return to you. Encouraging you, sending you ideas, resources and energy. Give the positive energy that HOPE carries and HOPE will fill your soul.

Day One (Week 10)
Growing My Wealth With Hope

Read this out loud when you arise; from "I promise to" through "I always keep my promises". Be certain to sign it and include your name in the reading out loud.

I promise to follow these 4 steps today

1. I read the First Verity two times today, first thing in the morning and aloud in the evening just before I go to bed.

2. I read my "Intention" card three times today with enthusiasm

3. I encourage at least one person today

4. As I go through my day, I identify hope everywhere

_____

I always keep my promises

Here are a few examples of hope. Compliments, people helping people, advice with no motive, encouragement, compassion, empathy. Note each one and check off a box for each example you find during the day. Find some of your own! The more examples of kindness you identify, the kinder becomes the world and you realize how everything that is good is also incredibly abundant.

OOOOO OOOOO OOOOO OOOOO OOOOO

Before your nighttime read and sitting still, check off the examples you saw. Each day the number you spot will grow if you focus.

Jot down the best example you observed today of hope.

Day Two (Week 10)
Growing My Wealth With Hope

Read this out loud when you arise; from "I promise to" through "I always keep my promises". Be certain to sign it and include your name in the reading out loud.

I promise to follow these 4 steps today

1. *I read the Second Verity two times today, first thing in the morning and aloud in the evening just before I go to bed.*

2. *I read my "Intention" card three times today with enthusiasm*

3. *I encourage at least one person today*

4. *As I go through my day, I identify hope everywhere*

I always keep my promises

Here are a few examples of hope. Compliments, people helping people, advice with no motive, encouragement, compassion, empathy. Note each one and check off a box for each example you find during the day. Find some of your own! The more examples of kindness you identify, the kinder becomes the world and you realize how everything that is good is also incredibly abundant.

○○○○○ ○○○○○ ○○○○○ ○○○○○ ○○○○○

Before your nighttime read and sitting still, check off the examples you saw. Each day the number you spot will grow if you focus.

Jot down the best example you observed today of hope.

Day Three (Week 10)
Growing My Wealth With Hope

Read this out loud when you arise; from "I promise to" through "I always keep my promises". Be certain to sign it and include your name in the reading out loud.

I promise to follow these 4 steps today

1. I read the Third Verity two times today, first thing in the morning and aloud in the evening just before I go to bed.

2. I read my "Intention" card three times today with enthusiasm

3. I encourage at least one person today

4. As I go through my day, I identify hope everywhere

_____

I always keep my promises

Here are a few examples of hope. Compliments, people helping people, advice with no motive, encouragement, compassion, empathy. Note each one and check off a box for each example you find during the day. Find some of your own! The more examples of kindness you identify, the kinder becomes the world and you realize how everything that is good is also incredibly abundant.

○○○○○ ○○○○○ ○○○○○ ○○○○○ ○○○○○

Before your nighttime read and sitting still, check off the examples you saw. Each day the number you spot will grow if you focus.
Jot down the best example you observed today of hope.

Day Four (Week 10)
Growing My Wealth With Hope

Read this out loud when you arise; from "I promise to" through "I always keep my promises". Be certain to sign it and include your name in the reading out loud.

I promise to follow these 4 steps today

1. I read the Fourth Verity two times today, first thing in the morning and aloud in the evening just before I go to bed.

2. I read my "Intention" card three times today with enthusiasm

3. I encourage at least one person today

4. As I go through my day, I identify hope everywhere

_____

I always keep my promises

Here are a few examples of hope. Compliments, people helping people, advice with no motive, encouragement, compassion, empathy. Note each one and check off a box for each example you find during the day. Find some of your own! The more examples of kindness you identify, the kinder becomes the world and you realize
how everything that is good is also incredibly abundant.

○○○○○ ○○○○○ ○○○○○ ○○○○○ ○○○○○

Before your nighttime read and sitting still, check off the examples you saw. Each day the number you spot will grow if you focus.
Jot down the best example you observed today of hope.

Day Five (Week 10)
Growing My Wealth With Hope

Read this out loud when you arise; from "I promise to" through "I always keep my promises". Be certain to sign it and include your name in the reading out loud.

I promise to follow these 4 steps today

1. I read the Fifth Verity two times today, first thing in the morning and aloud in the evening just before I go to bed.

2. I read my "Intention" card three times today with enthusiasm

3. I encourage at least one person today

4. As I go through my day, I identify hope everywhere

_____

I always keep my promises

Here are a few examples of hope. Compliments, people helping people, advice with no motive, encouragement, compassion, empathy. Note each one and check off a box for each example you find during the day. Find some of your own! The more examples of kindness you identify, the kinder becomes the world and you realize how everything that is good is also incredibly abundant.

○○○○○　○○○○○　○○○○○　○○○○○　○○○○○

Before your nighttime read and sitting still, check off the examples you saw. Each day the number you spot will grow if you focus.
Jot down the best example you observed today of hope.

Day Six (Week 10)
Growing My Wealth With Hope

Read this out loud when you arise; from "I promise to" through "I always keep my promises". Be certain to sign it and include your name in the reading out loud.

I promise to follow these 4 steps today

1. I read the Sixth Verity two times today, first thing in the morning and aloud in the evening just before I go to bed.

2. I read my "Intention" card three times today with enthusiasm

3. I encourage at least one person today

4. As I go through my day, I identify hope everywhere

_____

I always keep my promises

Here are a few examples of hope. Compliments, people helping people, advice with no motive, encouragement, compassion, empathy. Note each one and check off a box for each example you find during the day. Find some of your own! The more examples of kindness you identify, the kinder becomes the world and you realize how everything that is good is also incredibly abundant.

○○○○○ ○○○○○ ○○○○○ ○○○○○ ○○○○○

Before your nighttime read and sitting still, check off the examples you saw. Each day the number you spot will grow if you focus.
Jot down the best example you observed today of hope.

Day Seven (Week 10)
Growing My Wealth With Hope

Read this out loud when you arise; from "I promise to" through "I always keep my promises". Be certain to sign it and include your name in the reading out loud.

I promise to follow these 4 steps today

1. I read the Seventh Verity two times today, first thing in the morning and aloud in the evening just before I go to bed.

2. I read my "Intention" card three times today with enthusiasm

3. I encourage at least one person today

4. As I go through my day, I identify hope everywhere

_____

I always keep my promises

Here are a few examples of hope. Compliments, people helping people, advice with no motive, encouragement, compassion, empathy. Note each one and check off a box for each example you find during the day. Find some of your own! The more examples of kindness you identify, the kinder becomes the world and you realize how everything that is good is also incredibly abundant.

○○○○○   ○○○○○   ○○○○○   ○○○○○   ○○○○○

Before your nighttime read and sitting still, check off the examples you saw. Each day the number you spot will grow if you focus.
Jot down the best example you observed today of hope.

The Eleventh of the 13 Riches
Willingness to Share Blessings

As wealth pours into your life in all areas, your willingness to share the blessings will determine the authentic value they carry to you. Many have wealth but do not live by the principles of The Verities. They do not enjoy their wealth and trap themselves into thinking that more things will make them feel safe and secure. What good is wealth if one does not enjoy it? What pleasure is there in having more wealth than one could ever use if all their time is spent in worry about losing it? Such is the fate of those who lack the willingness to share their blessings.

From the very First Verity, you have turned yourself into a grateful giver and a humble receiver. As you use the Law of Growth to build wealth, your willingness to share your blessings becomes the key to unlimited wealth. To become the Richest in all areas of life and never have a worry about more pouring in is found within your willingness to share all your blessings. Some are selective about what they share. Eventually, what they keep begins to own them, to possess them, to rule them. This is not true wealth. To trigger an endless flow of wealth, we must be willing to share all our blessings, not a select few. Throughout time we have learned that the greatest blessing, the authentic connection to others, is the most elusive one. All men and all women share the desire to have honest relationships. Sharing your money, your positive mental attitude and your kindness are wonderful but are you willing to share your greatest blessing? Yourself?

Become transparent to all. Share your dreams, your hopes and your fears. Share your mistakes, share your heartaches, share your wisdom, share your weaknesses and feelings. For the blessing of who you really are will encourage others to be themselves. And the richness of an honest, transparent relationship carries a wealth that transcends all things.

How?

Just as the world is perfect yet incomplete, so are we. Within these transparent relationships between two people surface the ways and means for them both to be perfect. The willingness to share blessings, all of them, is the determining factor in the value they have to you. Great willingness produces great con-fidence and massive abundance. Willingness to share everything, including you, is the only pathway to true love.

Day One (Week 11)
Growing My Wealth With The Willingness to Share Blessings

Read this out loud when you arise; from "I promise to" through "I always keep my promises". Be certain to sign it and include your name in the reading out loud.

I promise to follow these 3 steps today

1. *I read the First Verity two times today, first thing in the morning and aloud in the evening just before I go to bed.*

2. *I read my "Intention" card three times today with enthusiasm*

3. *As I go through my day, I identify sharing*

_____

I always keep my promises

Here are a few examples of sharing blessings. Offering time, giving without being asked, sharing a drink, a meal, a story, a book, information, giving time. Note each one and check off a box for each example you find during the day. Find some of your own! The more you identify sharing and transparency the more others will share with you and the harmony you've been striving for in all relationships will transform into love.

○○○○○ ○○○○○ ○○○○○ ○○○○○ ○○○○○

Before your nighttime read and sitting still, check off the examples you saw. Each day the number you spot will grow if you focus.
Jot down the best example you observed today of sharing.

Day Two (Week 11)
Growing My Wealth With The Willingness to Share Blessings

Read this out loud when you arise; from "I promise to" through "I always keep my promises". Be certain to sign it and include your name in the reading out loud.

I promise to follow these 3 steps today

1. I read the Second Verity two times today, first thing in the morning and aloud in the evening just before I go to bed.

2. I read my "Intention" card three times today with enthusiasm

3. As I go through my day, I identify sharing

_____

I always keep my promises

Here are a few examples of sharing blessings. Offering time, giving without being asked, sharing a drink, a meal, time, a story, a book, information. Note each one and check off a box for each example you find during the day. Find some of your own! The more you identify sharing and transparency the more others will share with you and the harmony you've been striving for in all relationships will transform into love..

O O O O O   O O O O O   O O O O O   O O O O O   O O O O O

Before your nighttime read and sitting still, check off the examples you saw. Each day the number you spot will grow if you focus.
Jot down the best example you observed today of sharing.

Day Three (Week 11)
Growing My Wealth With The Willingness to Share Blessings

Read this out loud when you arise; from "I promise to" through "I always keep my promises". Be certain to sign it and include your name in the reading out loud.

I promise to follow these 3 steps today

1. I read the Third Verity two times today, first thing in the morning and aloud in the evening just before I go to bed.

2. I read my "Intention" card three times today with enthusiasm

3. As I go through my day, I identify sharing

_____

I always keep my promises

Here are a few examples of sharing blessings. Offering time, giving without being asked, sharing a drink, a meal, time, a story, a book, information. Note each one and check off a box for each example you find during the day. Find some of your own! The more you identify sharing and transparency the more others will share with you and the harmony you've been striving for in all relationships will transform into love..

OOOOO   OOOOO   OOOOO   OOOOO   OOOOO

Before your nighttime read and sitting still, check off the examples you saw. Each day the number you spot will grow if you focus.
Jot down the best example you observed today of sharing.

Day Four (Week 11)
Growing My Wealth With The Willingness to Share Blessings

Read this out loud when you arise; from "I promise to" through "I always keep my promises". Be certain to sign it and include your name in the reading out loud.

I promise to follow these 3 steps today

1. *I read the Fourth Verity two times today, first thing in the morning and aloud in the evening just before I go to bed.*

2. *I read my "Intention" card three times today with enthusiasm*

3. *As I go through my day, I identify sharing*

_____

I always keep my promises

Here are a few examples of sharing blessings. Offering time, giving without being asked, sharing a drink, a meal, time, a story, a book, information. Note each one and check off a box for each example you find during the day. Find some of your own! The more you identify sharing and transparency the more others will share with you and the harmony you've been striving for in all relationships will transform into love..

○○○○○ ○○○○○ ○○○○○ ○○○○○ ○○○○○

Before your nighttime read and sitting still, check off the examples you saw. Each day the number you spot will grow if you focus.
Jot down the best example you observed today of sharing.

Day Five (Week 11)
Growing My Wealth With The Willingness to Share Blessings

Read this out loud when you arise; from "I promise to" through "I always keep my promises". Be certain to sign it and include your name in the reading out loud.

I promise to follow these 3 steps today

1. *I read the Fifth Verity two times today, first thing in the morning and aloud in the evening just before I go to bed.*

2. *I read my "Intention" card three times today with enthusiasm*

3. *As I go through my day, I identify sharing*

_____

I always keep my promises

Here are a few examples of sharing blessings. Offering time, giving without being asked, sharing a drink, a meal, time, a story, a book, information. Note each one and check off a box for each example you find during the day. Find some of your own! The more you identify sharing and transparency the more others will share with you and the harmony you've been striving for in all relationships will transform into love..

○○○○○ ○○○○○ ○○○○○ ○○○○○ ○○○○○

Before your nighttime read and sitting still, check off the examples you saw. Each day the number you spot will grow if you focus.
Jot down the best example you observed today of sharing.

186

Day Six (Week 11)
Growing My Wealth With The Willingness to Share Blessings

Read this out loud when you arise; from "I promise to" through "I always keep my promises". Be certain to sign it and include your name in the reading out loud.

I promise to follow these 3 steps today

1. I read the Sixth Verity two times today, first thing in the morning and aloud in the evening just before I go to bed.

2. I read my "Intention" card three times today with enthusiasm

3. As I go through my day, I identify sharing

_____

I always keep my promises

Here are a few examples of sharing blessings. Offering time, giving without being asked, sharing a drink, a meal, time, a story, a book, information. Note each one and check off a box for each example you find during the day. Find some of your own! The more you identify sharing and transparency the more others will share with you and the harmony you've been striving for in all relationships will transform into love..

○○○○○ ○○○○○ ○○○○○ ○○○○○ ○○○○○

Before your nighttime read and sitting still, check off the examples you saw. Each day the number you spot will grow if you focus.
Jot down the best example you observed today of sharing.

187

Day Seven (Week 11)
Growing My Wealth With The Willingness to Share Blessings

Read this out loud when you arise; from "I promise to" through "I always keep my promises". Be certain to sign it and include your name in the reading out loud.

I promise to follow these 3 steps today

1. I read the Seventh Verity two times today, first thing in the morning and aloud in the evening just before I go to bed.

2. I read my "Intention" card three times today with enthusiasm

3. As I go through my day, I identify sharing

_____

I always keep my promises

Here are a few examples of sharing blessings. Offering time, giving without being asked, sharing a drink, a meal, time, a story, a book, information. Note each one and check off a box for each example you find during the day. Find some of your own! The more you identify sharing and transparency the more others will share with you and the harmony you've been striving for in all relationships will transform into love..

○○○○○ ○○○○○ ○○○○○ ○○○○○ ○○○○○

Before your nighttime read and sitting still, check off the examples you saw. Each day the number you spot will grow if you focus.
Jot down the best example you observed today of sharing.

The Twelfth of the 13 Riches
Play

For thousands of years before and most likely for thousands of years to come, people lament the speed of life. Elders try to impress the youth with their feelings of how short life is and the youth ignore them... only to turn into the elders themselves and communicating the same message in vain too.

And no one gets to the end of a life and regrets not working harder. Rather, with much pain, they moan about moments with family they missed to work, adventures they procrastinated about and never got to experience, wonders they missed and laughter that was experienced far to little.

The Riches of Play will be richer than you can imagine. Since you have mastered the Fifth Verity and now keep first things first, engaging in play, fun and frolicking like a child shall ignite happiness in your heart. There is a season for everything in the cycle of life; a season to plant, a season to grow, a season to harvest and a season to let the land replenish itself. Let nature be your teacher. Know that when you have fun, when you play and experience adventure, your body, mind and spirit become replenished. This will make you better at everything. This carries a greater lesson and is one of the secrets of The Map. Play like a child and learn from children. As you strive to be transparent, you will come to know that the very best teachers of honesty, of transparency and of being themselves are children. Notice how they carry no self-consciousness and how honest they are. Let their lessons, delivered without doubt, flow into you. Carry them with you to the world.

For just as we all love seeing children play, we must remember that all people yearn for playfulness, humor and relief from daily burdens. As you absorb this priceless lesson from children and friends who enjoy playing, keep giving it away. While the journey is important and the cause to improve the world you live in is vital, let's not forget there is nothing so funny as a person who believes she is too important to play.

Day One (Week 12)
Growing My Wealth with Play

Read this out loud when you arise; from "I promise to" through "I always keep my promises". Be certain to sign it and include your name in the reading out loud.

I promise to follow these 3 steps today

1. I read the First Verity two times today, first thing in the morning and aloud in the evening just before I go to bed.

2. I read my "Intention" card three times today with enthusiasm

3. As I go through my day, I identify playing

_____

I always keep my promises

Here are a few examples of playing. Singing, dancing, games, athletics, sport, puzzles, jokes, humor, laughter. Note each one and check off a box for each example you find during the day. Find some of your own! The more you identify play the more chances you will have to play and the less self-conscious and more refreshed you become.

OOOOO OOOOO OOOOO OOOOO OOOOO

Before your nighttime read and sitting still, check off the examples you saw. Each day the number you spot will grow if you focus.
Jot down the best example you observed today of play.

Day Two (Week 12)
Growing My Wealth with Play

Read this out loud when you arise; from "I promise to" through "I always keep my promises". Be certain to sign it and include your name in the reading out loud.

I promise to follow these 3 steps today

1. I read the Second Verity two times today, first thing in the morning and aloud in the evening just before I go to bed.

2. I read my "Intention" card three times today with enthusiasm

3. As I go through my day, I identify playing

_____

I always keep my promises

Here are a few examples of playing. Singing, dancing, games, athletics, sport, puzzles, jokes, humor, laughter. Note each one and check off a box for each example you find during the day. Find some of your own! The more you identify play the more chances you will have to play and the less self-conscious and more refreshed you become.

○○○○○ ○○○○○ ○○○○○ ○○○○○ ○○○○○

Before your nighttime read and sitting still, check off the examples you saw. Each day the number you spot will grow if you focus.

Jot down the best example you observed today of play.

Day Three (Week 12)
Growing My Wealth with Play

Read this out loud when you arise; from "I promise to" through "I always keep my promises". Be certain to sign it and include your name in the reading out loud.

I promise to follow these 3 steps today

1. I read the Third Verity two times today, first thing in the morning and aloud in the evening just before I go to bed.

2. I read my "Intention" card three times today with enthusiasm

3. As I go through my day, I identify playing

_____

I always keep my promises

Here are a few examples of playing. Singing, dancing, games, athletics, sport, puzzles, jokes, humor, laughter. Note each one and check off a box for each example you find during the day. Find some of your own! The more you identify play the more chances you will have to play and the less self-conscious and more refreshed you become.

○○○○○ ○○○○○ ○○○○○ ○○○○○ ○○○○○

Before your nighttime read and sitting still, check off the examples you saw. Each day the number you spot will grow if you focus.

Jot down the best example you observed today of play.

Day Four (Week 12)
Growing My Wealth with Play

Read this out loud when you arise; from "I promise to" through "I always keep my promises". Be certain to sign it and include your name in the reading out loud.

I promise to follow these 3 steps today

1. I read the Fourth Verity two times today, first thing in the morning and aloud in the evening just before I go to bed.

2. I read my "Intention" card three times today with enthusiasm

3. As I go through my day, I identify playing

_____

I always keep my promises

Here are a few examples of playing. Singing, dancing, games, athletics, sport, puzzles, jokes, humor, laughter. Note each one and check off a box for each example you find during the day. Find some of your own! The more you identify play the more chances you will have to play and the less self-conscious and more refreshed you become.

○○○○○　○○○○○　○○○○○　○○○○○　○○○○○

Before your nighttime read and sitting still, check off the examples you saw. Each day the number you spot will grow if you focus.
Jot down the best example you observed today of play.

Day Five (Week 12)
Growing My Wealth with Play

Read this out loud when you arise; from "I promise to" through "I always keep my promises". Be certain to sign it and include your name in the reading out loud.

I promise to follow these 3 steps today

1. I read the Fifth Verity two times today, first thing in the morning and aloud in the evening just before I go to bed.

2. I read my "Intention" card three times today with enthusiasm

3. As I go through my day, I identify playing

_____

I always keep my promises

Here are a few examples of playing. Singing, dancing, games, athletics, sport, puzzles, jokes, humor, laughter. Note each one and check off a box for each example you find during the day. Find some of your own! The more you identify play the more chances you will have to play and the less self-conscious and more refreshed you become.

O O O O O   O O O O O   O O O O O   O O O O O   O O O O O

Before your nighttime read and sitting still, check off the examples you saw. Each day the number you spot will grow if you focus.

Jot down the best example you observed today of play.

Day Six (Week 12)
Growing My Wealth with Play

Read this out loud when you arise; from "I promise to" through "I always keep my promises". Be certain to sign it and include your name in the reading out loud.

I promise to follow these 3 steps today

1. I read the Sixth Verity two times today, first thing in the morning and aloud in the evening just before I go to bed.

2. I read my "Intention" card three times today with enthusiasm

3. As I go through my day, I identify playing

_____

I always keep my promises

Here are a few examples of playing. Singing, dancing, games, athletics, sport, puzzles, jokes, humor, laughter. Note each one and check off a box for each example you find during the day. Find some of your own! The more you identify play the more chances you will have to play and the less self-conscious and more refreshed you become.

OOOOO OOOOO OOOOO OOOOO OOOOO

Before your nighttime read and sitting still, check off the examples you saw. Each day the number you spot will grow if you focus.
Jot down the best example you observed today of play.

Day Seven (Week 12)
Growing My Wealth with Play

Read this out loud when you arise; from "I promise to" through "I always keep my promises". Be certain to sign it and include your name in the reading out loud.

I promise to follow these 3 steps today

1. I read the Seventh Verity two times today, first thing in the morning and aloud in the evening just before I go to bed.

2. I read my "Intention" card three times today with enthusiasm

3. As I go through my day, I identify playing

_____

I always keep my promises

Here are a few examples of playing. Singing, dancing, games, athletics, sport, puzzles, jokes, humor, laughter. Note each one and check off a box for each example you find during the day. Find some of your own! The more you identify play the more chances you will have to play and the less self-conscious and more refreshed you become.

〇〇〇〇〇　〇〇〇〇〇　〇〇〇〇〇　〇〇〇〇〇　〇〇〇〇〇

Before your nighttime read and sitting still, check off the examples you saw. Each day the number you spot will grow if you focus.
Jot down the best example you observed today of play.

The Thirteenth of the 13 Riches
Sound Financial Wealth

It is not that financially prosperous people do certain things; they just do things in a "Certain Way". The wonderful news is that you have learned this "Certain Way" through the Verities. All that is left to do is understand what you already know, as it applies to business.

Three merchants sell rugs in the market place. The quality of the carpets is about the same. The price they are charging is about the same. Within three years, one has failed, one barely makes a living and one has become financially rich. The rich one simply did things in a "Certain Way". What is that "Certain Way"?

When asked, the failed merchant and the one who struggles thought of profit instead of their prospects best interests and needs. The "Certain Way" is to collaborate with prospects, not simply sell and service them. The financially rich only engage in transactions that benefit all, and most of all, the customer. They see it as an honor to be of service, to find out what their customer needs and make certain it fits the customer's budget. They send some customers to competitors if the competitor has a better match for that customer's need. As a result, the customers he does obtain cannot help but recommend this merchant to everyone.

To have financial wealth, one must live the principles of the Verities and share all the riches, like kindness, hope and a positive mental attitude with potential customers. Remember willingness to share blessings? Do it. The "Certain Way" is to let the Seven Verities be what you are, let them shine through and above all, to be really rich financially, you must not be like the monkey refusing to let go of the banana when it comes to money. Those who do things a "Certain Way" have long let go of the idea that more for someone else means less for them. Understand abundance by contemplating all the stars, the grains of sand on all the beaches and deserts. The Source of All Good designed us to grow. Those who do things a "Certain Way" do not think there is a limit to things. Rather, they think the way they were designed; to grow and to help create increase. They think increase. Financial wealth? Observe abundance. Think increase. Only think increase. Success is service.

Day One (Week 13)
Growing My Wealth with Play

Read this out loud when you arise; from "I promise to" through "I always keep my promises". Be certain to sign it and include your name in the reading out loud.

I promise to follow these 4 steps today

1. I read the First Verity two times today, first thing in the morning and aloud in the evening just before I go to bed.

2. I read my "Intention" card three times today with enthusiasm

3. I repeat "I see abundance everywhere" 20 times per day for this week

4. As I go through my day, I identify transactions and customers well served

---

I always keep my promises

Here are a few examples of service transactions. Busy merchants, goods and services moving, people buying, clothes and transportation people use, workers, service people. Note each one and check off a box for each example you find during the day. Find some of your own! The more transactions and those who do them successfully you identify, the more chances to serve and earn will cascade into your life. You increase financial success with the same Law of Growth as usual.

○○○○○ ○○○○○ ○○○○○ ○○○○○ ○○○○○

Before your nighttime read and sitting still, check off the examples you saw. Each day the number you spot will grow if you focus.

Jot down the best example you observed today of a successful service.

Day Two (Week 13)
Growing My Wealth with Play

Read this out loud when you arise; from "I promise to" through "I always keep my promises". Be certain to sign it and include your name in the reading out loud.

I promise to follow these 4 steps today

1. I read the Second Verity two times today, first thing in the morning and aloud in the evening just before I go to bed.

2. I read my "Intention" card three times today with enthusiasm

3. I repeat "I see abundance everywhere" 20 times per day for this week

4. As I go through my day, I identify transactions and customers well served

_____

I always keep my promises

Here are a few examples of service transactions. Busy merchants, goods and services moving, people buying, the clothes and transportation people use, workers, service people. Note each one and check off a box for each example you find during the day. Find some of your own! The more you identify the thousands of transactions and those who do it successfully; the more chances to serve and earn will cascade into your life. You increase financial success with the same Law of Growth as usual.

OOOOO OOOOO OOOOO OOOOO OOOOO

Before your nighttime read and sitting still, check off the examples you saw. Each day the number you spot will grow if you focus.

Jot down the best example you observed today of a successful service.

Day Three (Week 13)
Growing My Wealth with Play

Read this out loud when you arise; from "I promise to" through "I always keep my promises". Be certain to sign it and include your name in the reading out loud.

I promise to follow these 4 steps today

1. I read the Third Verity two times today, first thing in the morning and aloud in the evening just before I go to bed.

2. I read my "Intention" card three times today with enthusiasm

3. I repeat "I see abundance everywhere" 20 times per day for this week

4. As I go through my day, I identify transactions and customers well served

_____

I always keep my promises

Here are a few examples of service transactions. Busy merchants, goods and services moving, people buying, clothes and transportation people use, workers, service people. Note each one and check off a box for each example you find during the day. Find some of your own! The more transactions and those who do them successfully you identify, the more chances to serve and earn will cascade into your life. You increase financial success with the same Law of Growth as usual.

○○○○○ ○○○○○ ○○○○○ ○○○○○ ○○○○○

Before your nighttime read and sitting still, check off the examples you saw. Each day the number you spot will grow if you focus.
Jot down the best example you observed today of a successful service.

Day Four (Week 13)
Growing My Wealth with Play

Read this out loud when you arise; from "I promise to" through "I always keep my promises". Be certain to sign it and include your name in the reading out loud.

I promise to follow these 4 steps today

1. I read the Fourth Verity two times today, first thing in the morning and aloud in the evening just before I go to bed.

2. I read my "Intention" card three times today with enthusiasm

3. I repeat "I see abundance everywhere" 20 times per day for this week

4. As I go through my day, I identify transactions and customers well served

_____

I always keep my promises

Here are a few examples of service transactions. Busy merchants, goods and services moving, people buying, the clothes and transportation people use, workers, service people. Note each one and check off a box for each example you find during the day. Find some of your own! The more you identify the thousands of transactions and those who do it successfully; the more chances to serve and earn will cascade into your life. You increase financial success with the same Law of Growth as usual.

○○○○○ ○○○○○ ○○○○○ ○○○○○ ○○○○○

Before your nighttime read and sitting still, check off the examples you saw. Each day the number you spot will grow if you focus.

Jot down the best example you observed today of a successful service.

Day Five (Week 13)
Growing My Wealth with Play

Read this out loud when you arise; from "I promise to" through "I always keep my promises". Be certain to sign it and include your name in the reading out loud.

I promise to follow these 4 steps today

1. I read the Fifth Verity two times today, first thing in the morning and aloud in the evening just before I go to bed.

2. I read my "Intention" card three times today with enthusiasm

3. I repeat "I see abundance everywhere" 20 times per day for this week

4. As I go through my day, I identify transactions and customers well served

_____

I always keep my promises

Here are a few examples of service transactions. Busy merchants, goods and services moving, people buying, clothes and transportation people use, workers, service people. Note each one and check off a box for each example you find during the day. Find some of your own! The more transactions and those who do them successfully you identify, the more chances to serve and earn will cascade into your life. You increase financial success with the same Law of Growth as usual.

○○○○○ ○○○○○ ○○○○○ ○○○○○ ○○○○○

Before your nighttime read and sitting still, check off the examples you saw. Each day the number you spot will grow if you focus.

Jot down the best example you observed today of a successful service.

Day Six (Week 13)
Growing My Wealth with Play

Read this out loud when you arise; from "I promise to" through "I always keep my promises". Be certain to sign it and include your name in the reading out loud.

I promise to follow these 4 steps today

1. *I read the Sixth Verity two times today, first thing in the morning and aloud in the evening just before I go to bed.*

2. *I read my "Intention" card three times today with enthusiasm*

3. *I repeat "I see abundance everywhere" 20 times per day for this week*

4. *As I go through my day, I identify transactions and customers well served*

_____

I always keep my promises

Here are a few examples of service transactions. Busy merchants, goods and services moving, people buying, the clothes and transportation people use, workers, service people. Note each one and check off a box for each example you find during the day. Find some of your own! The more you identify the thousands of transactions and those who do it successfully; the more chances to serve and earn will cascade into your life. You increase financial success with the same Law of Growth as usual.

O O O O O   O O O O O   O O O O O   O O O O O   O O O O O

Before your nighttime read and sitting still, check off the examples you saw. Each day the number you spot will grow if you focus.

Jot down the best example you observed today of a successful service.

Day Seven (Week 13)
Growing My Wealth with Play

Read this out loud when you arise; from "I promise to" through "I always keep my promises". Be certain to sign it and include your name in the reading out loud.

I promise to follow these 4 steps today

1. I read the Seventh Verity two times today, first thing in the morning and aloud in the evening just before I go to bed.
2. I read my "Intention" card three times today with enthusiasm
3. I repeat "I see abundance everywhere" 20 times per day for this week
4. As I go through my day, I identify transactions and customers well served

_____

I always keep my promises

Here are a few examples of service transactions. Busy merchants, goods and services moving, people buying, clothes and transportation people use, workers, service people. Note each one and check off a box for each example you find during the day. Find some of your own! The more transactions and those who do them successfully you identify, the more chances to serve and earn will cascade into your life. You increase financial success with the same Law of Growth as usual.

○○○○○　○○○○○　○○○○○　○○○○○　○○○○○

Before your nighttime read and sitting still, check off the examples you saw. Each day the number you spot will grow if you focus.

Jot down the best example you observed today of a successful service.

206

The Choice

There once was a hall that held great artifacts from the four corners of the world. People traveled from near and far to see the many wonders. One exhibit held two large dinosaur eggs and was always the most crowded. People were fascinated by this great exhibition. What the viewers never realized was that the eggs, to both the mothers and the unborn dinosaurs, represented a complete and utter failure. The same fate becomes true of The Map, if you simply let it sit there after completing it the first time.

The Map will yield new insights begetting untold wealth to those who return to the first of the riches, A Positive Mental Attitude, and begin the journey again with greater enthusiasm. The Map promises and delivers even more wealth each time you work through the 13 Riches. Unlike a mine of gold or silver, the deeper you dig, the more focused you become, the more The Map will surrender in both wisdom and wealth.

This then becomes The Choice all who have held The Map face; to work through The Map again with greater precision or to lay it down, let it gather dust and wait for someone worthy to pass on The Verities and The Map by hand. Those who become wealthy beyond measure are they who have established their own values, measuring not by what they acquire but rather by what they contribute. The more wealth you acquire, the more you have to give. The more often you journey within and use The Map to guide you, the grander the gifts and wealth you have to share. And as what we give returns in even greater quantities, what you have to give compounds as do your contributions.

Your greatest contribution will be when the time comes to pass The Verities and The Map to the 13 Riches exactly as you received them to someone who is worthy.

And how will you know if someone is worthy? When you become humbled by the flow of blessings beyond comprehension that pour into your life daily. This happens when you surrender to the truth that the infinite is in the finite, when you are totally immersed in each and every moment as a way of life. When you live in this level of total consciousness and know everything is connected and so are you, the next worthy recipient, a person of honor who keeps their promises, will find you, will chose you. You need not seek them and the truth you need to make the correct choice will dance in your heart.

Keep giving to keep growing.

Chapter Fifteen

"A Sort of a Book thing"

Igot to the Seattle Zoo around 11:30. I figured that Doc would show up right around noon. I was wrong; he was sitting there, looking, of

course, at the giraffes. We hugged, long and intense.

"See that one, the playful one?" I nodded. "That's Fola," Doc said. He wore the same childlike enthusiasm I had witnessed back in Oakland.

"I meant to ask you when we were in Oakland if that giraffe was really named Joey."

"Does it matter?" Doc asked, winking. "No, not really, just curious." I said.

"I don't know if they even have names. I never asked. I just named them myself. Joey is my brother, actually Joe, but that giraffe was young when I adopted him, so Joey just seemed right, ya know? Now Fola, well, I thought an African name might be nice. In Nigeria, that name means 'honor' and keeping our promises, well, you know..." Doc's voice trailed off.

He pointed to a bench, and we walked over. "We got unfinished business about the *sort of a book thing*, but I want to hear about your wealth and what you'll do next, the choice you made."

I shared with Doc some of the blessings that had been cascading into my life from channels I had never expected, never even knew existed; the huge influx of people reading my blog, two articles major magazines paid me for, an advance from a publisher for a book of short stories... I started choking up a few minutes into my story. Doc put his hand over my face, covering my whole face gently as I composed myself.

"I don't need to know anymore," he said softly. "And the choice? What are you going to do next?" I let him know that I had already started the first of the 13 Riches again. He nodded and told me that he hadn't missed a day in years.

"Doc, all your emails are signed *'keep giving to keep growing'*, and I was wondering if you got that off the last page of The Map, or if you added it." I figured he'd ask, "does it matter?" Sure enough, he did, accompanied by another wink and a smile.

We got a couple hot dogs, and he brought up our unfinished business. "Each person who gets these Verities at the turn of a millennium decides to write them out by hand and pass them to an individual or bring them to the world. So, let's talk about the 'sort of a book thing' and figure out what to do together."

We talked the afternoon away, but most of the conversation centered on Doc's first meeting with Toni and Peter, actually something I remembered he'd told me they had said to him about love. And Johannes Gutenberg. We talked a lot about Gutenberg's invention of the printing press.

"As I recall, Toni had said to you something like, *love is in need of love*, and they wanted you to bring The Verities to the world because of that. What do you think she meant?" I asked.

"I'm not sure, what it meant specifically to her. We've talked about it a few times. I think people who go through the Verities and the Map, who really follow the directions, would agree that connecting with *The Source of All Good* is really a highly individualized experience, unique for each of us. Our understanding of what Source is, also differs; calling it *The Source*, God, Jesus, Universal Mind, Allah, Creator... I really believe the one commonality is that when we realize we are channels, representatives of The Source, somehow, we experience its love. Maybe completely, maybe in part, but love seems to be the common denominator. Make sense?"

"I agree, Doc."

"So, it seems like we're always saying things like, *God bless you, or God bless America*, or whatever... Heal this ... Fix that ... Please, heal, Mary ...anyway, you get the idea. What if we reversed that and let The Source know of our love for it, sent our love, our blessings, and asked nothing in return? In other words, what if we even moved past thanking and started giving... all of us, our good wishes, our love, our blessings to The Source. Maybe we could start sending love back and initiating love to The Source, instead of directing The Source where we think it should send love and blessings."

We talked about that for a couple of hours before coming to the inevitable conclusion. *Why not just put the idea of blessing The Source with love into action and see what happens, instead of getting attached to what it might mean or the results that may come of it?*

On a hunch, I asked Doc if he was already doing that, blessing The Source... and, of course, he grinned that now-familiar, impish yet peace-bearing grin and responded, "Does it matter?"

What *did* seem to matter to Doc was Johannes Gutenberg, or, at least, the burden of his invention, the printing press. Doc reminded me that people who get *the Verities and The Map* passed to them at the turn of the millennium are the ones who must decide to continue with the tradition of passing them intact to an individual or deciding to bring it to everyone, to the world.

"See, the interesting thing is that, up until now, right now, the capabilities to bring The Verities and The Map to the world on a large scale never existed for our predecessors who passed them as a millennium changed. The ritual has been to write them out by hand when the right person picks you. When you add in how many people couldn't read, well, ah... the passers never had a real burden. There was no way to do it, even if they wanted to, and, for the most part, people couldn't read."

"Do you really feel like it's a burden?" I asked.

"Maybe I'm just pretending it is," he admitted. "See, those giraffes know what they are supposed to do. Be a giraffe. Period. We get to make choices; they don't. I guess the right action already picked me back on my lanai the first time we hooked up in person. It was clear you would honor the promises you make. I guess where the struggle lives is in the not knowing."

"The not knowing?" I asked.

"I just don't know if writing this 'sort of a book thing' ... if that action picked you."

I smiled and asked, "Does it matter?"

Doc's head quickly snapped back from giraffe-gazing toward me. He gave me a gentle punch on my arm and warmly embraced me.

Post Script

An Invitation

Legend has it that, for centuries, an 8th Verity should be added, the "S" Verity. The idea has been that the "S" verity would stand for Sharing

Ideas. Over the centuries, sustained successes have had something in common. That commonality? A group of supportive people who will keep us on track with both purpose and plan. In his book, *Think and Grow Rich*, *Napoleon Hill popularized it with the term Mastermind Alliance.*

"No one makes it without a Mastermind Alliance, that's just the way it is."

—Napoleon Hill

Others' successes and positive ideas are priceless encouragements. So, we'd like to extend invitations to you to share your story. Please visit us— Doc and me—at http://markjbooks.com, and let us know about your experiences, strengths, and hopes as you traverse The Map.

There, you will discover groups who are working through *Standing Tall*. It really is easier to stay on track with plan and purpose when others are supporting you. The friendships and rich flow of ideas people experience is priceless when it is shared.

"What cannot be achieved in one lifetime will happen when one lifetime is joined to another."

—Harold Kushner

The Master Key Experience

Once a year, we offer a six-month Mastermind, The Master Key Experience, with people from around the world. While most declare that it is the most challenging thing they have ever undertaken, they also state, that it is, without a doubt, the best thing that they have ever done for themselves. Since you have purchased this book, you automatically receive a pay-it-forward scholarship to the course. That simply means that the previous sessions' members have "paid" for future members. If you'd like to be informed about the course and claim your scholarship, you'll discover everything you need at http://markjbooks.com.

We'd love to hear from you and how working The Map has impacted both yourself and the people in your world.

Made in the USA
Monee, IL
21 April 2021